T0361199

Central Europe in the Twentieth Century

Central Europe in the Twentieth Century

An Economic History Perspective

Edited by

ALICE TEICHOVA

Routledge
Taylor & Francis Group

LONDON AND NEW YORK

First published 1997 by SCOLAR Press and Ashgate Publishing

Reissued 2018 by Routledge
2 Park Square, Milton Park, Abingdon, Oxon OX14 4RN
711 Third Avenue, New York, NY 10017, USA

Routledge is an imprint of the Taylor & Francis Group, an informa business

Notice:
Product or corporate names may be trademarks or registered trademarks, and are used only for identification and explanation without intent to infringe.

Publisher's Note
The publisher has gone to great lengths to ensure the quality of this reprint but points out that some imperfections in the original copies may be apparent.

Disclaimer
The publisher has made every effort to trace copyright holders and welcomes correspondence from those they have been unable to contact.

A Library of Congress record exists under LC control number: 96039037

ISBN 13: 978-1-138-61257-0 (hbk)
ISBN 13: 978-0-429-46168-2 (ebk)

Contents

List of Tables

List of Figures and List of Maps

Figures

Maps

The publisher would like to thank David Turnock for providing Maps 2 and 4.

Notes on Contributors

Daniel Daianu is Chief Economist at the National Bank of Romania, President of the Romanian Institute of Free Enterprise (IRLI) and Chairman of the Romanian Economic Society (SOREC). His most recent book is (1996) *Economic Vitality and Viability. A Double Challenge for European Security.*

Michael Kaser is General Editor of the International Economic Association and Emeritus Fellow St. Antony's College, Oxford. He is honorary Professor in the Institute for German Studies, University of Birmingham. He published 20 books on Eastern Europe and the Soviet Union, among them as editor (1985-86), *The Economic History of Eastern Europe 1919-1975,* 3 vols., Oxford.

Václav Průcha is Professor of Economic History at the Economics University in Prague. He is President of the Czech Economic History Association. He has published numerous books and articles and edited seminal volumes on the development of the Czechoslovak economy under capitalism, socialism and post-communism.

Jörg Roesler is Professor of Economic History and member of the Leibniz Sozietät, Berlin. He is the author of books and articles on economic history of East Germany, including (1990), *Zwischen Plan und Markt. Die Wirtschaftsreform 1963-1970 in der DDR,* and 'The Rise and Fall of the Planned Economy in the German Democratic Republic, 1945-89' in: (1991), *German History,* 9/1. At present he is working on a history of innovation in East German industry.

Franjo Štiblar is Professor of Economics at the School of Law of the University of Ljubljana (Slovenia), Scientific Advisor at the Economics Institute and Chief Economist at Nova Ljubljanska banka. He is the author of books and articles on economics and economic history, including (1989), *External Indebtedness in Eastern Europe,* and (1992), *Report on evolving legal structure for the private sector in Slovenia,* The World Bank.

Henryk Szlajfer, PhD, is editor and author of books and articles on comparative history and economic development, including (1990), *Economic Nationalism in East-Central Europe and South America 1918-1939,* Geneva. At present he is the Director of the Department of Studies and Planning, and Research Fellow at the Institute of Political Studies, Polish Academy of Sciences.

Alice Teichova is Emeritus Professor of Economic History at the University of East Anglia, Honorary Fellow of Girton College, Cambridge and Visiting Research Associate of the London School of Economics and Political Science. Her publications include (1988), *The Czechoslovak Economy 1918-1980* and 'East-central and south-east Europe, 1919-1939' in: Mathias, P. & Pollard, S. (eds), (1989), *The Cambridge Economic History of*

Europe, vol. VIII, pp. 887-982. At present her research is concerned with the economic and political role of Austria in interwar Central Europe.

Fritz Weber is Reader in Economic History at the University of Salzburg and the Economics University of Vienna. He has published widely on economic and social history, including (1986), *Der Kalte Krieg in der SPÖ*.

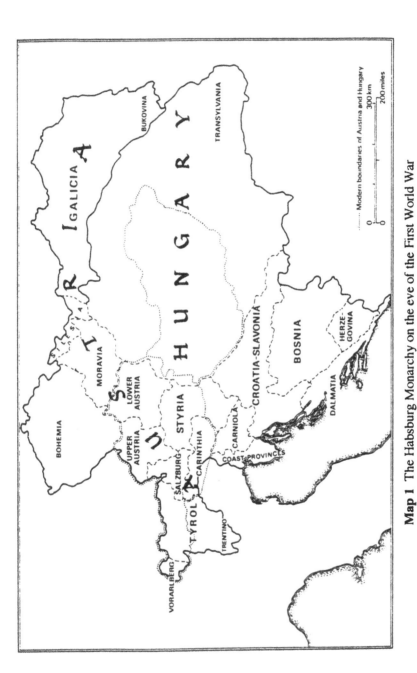

Map 1 The Habsburg Monarchy on the eve of the First World War

Source: Mathias, P. and Pollard, S. (eds.), *The Cambridge Economic History of Europe*, Vol. VIII, (Cambridge University Press, 1989), p.886

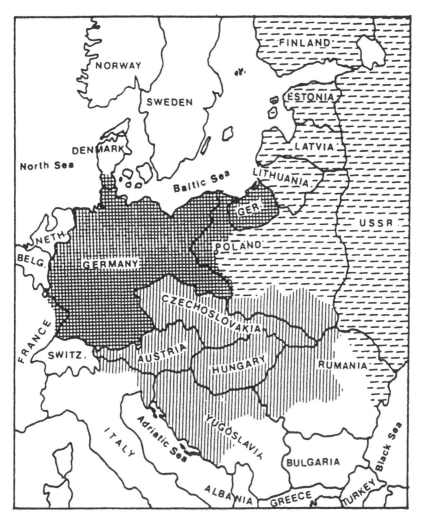

NORWAY

SWEDEN

DENMARK

North Sea

Baltic Sea

FINLAND

ESTONIA

LATVIA

LITHUANIA

GER.

POLAND

USSR

NETH.

BELG.

GERMANY

CZECHOSLOVAKIA

FRANCE

SWITZ.

AUSTRIA

HUNGARY

RUMANIA

ITALY

Adriatic Sea

YUGOSLAVIA

BULGARIA

Black Sea

ALBANIA

GREECE

TURKEY

 Former extent of Tsarist Russia

 Former extent of Austria-Hungary

 Former extent of the Second Reich

(Boundaries shown are those after the First World War)

Map 2 Europe 1923

xi

	Debt in convertible currency, 1984 (in dollars)	population 1983 (est.) (millions)
Albania	nil	2.9 (1982)
Bulgaria	560m	8.9
Czechoslovakia	3.6b	15.4
Hungary	7.6b	10.7
Poland	27b	36.7
Romania	7.2b	22.6
Yugoslavia	20b	22.8

Source: Barclays ABECOR Country Reports, 1984
The figures for foreign debts are estimates, and should be treated with caution.

Map 3 Central Europe 1978-9

Source: Okey, R., *Eastern Europe 1740 - 1980 Feudalism to Communism,*
(Hutchinson, London, 1982), p.217

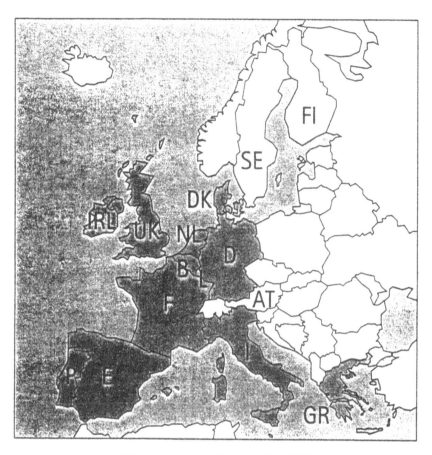

Map 4 European Community 1996

CHAPTER ONE

Introduction

Alice Teichova

It is dangerous to ignore history. Although the complicated threads connecting the past with the present are not always and everywhere immediately obvious, nevertheless their web exerts a powerful influence on contemporary events. However, the historical approach has largely gone out of fashion among economists and sociologists. Indeed, nearly all economists now reject historical methods of research, denying that lessons can be learnt from history. This especially applies to the economic advice the new elites in the Central and Southeast states have received on the immediate transition to the 'free market'. Such advice has tended to be divorced from both the realities of the 'actually existing capitalism' and the legacy of the shattered 'really existing socialism'.

This volume presents eight essays which attempt critically to assess the recent dramatic changes in Central and Southeast Europe within their historical context. At the same time the authors have sought to counterbalance the widespread impression of the whole area being a homogenous entity arising from an undifferentiated approach to those countries which had been part of the Soviet bloc. While these states geographically belong to Central and Southeast Europe, they have in the course of history, for reasons of power politics, continuously been shifted either to the West, the middle or the East of Europe. At the turn of the century the concept of *Mitteleuropa* was used to support German claims to territories east of her borders. After the break-up of the Austro-Hungarian Empire *Mitteleuropa* reappeared as a historically and politically amorphous and debatable concept. In addition to irrationally and nostalgically sanctioning the still lingering misconception of the conjured-up images of Central Europe's 'bridging' functions between West and East. Recently publicists have taken up this theme again and, according to their nationality or allegiance, we find that individual Central European states, or nations, or capital cities have laid claims to having performed this function from time immemorial to the present day (e.g. Poland, Bohemia and later Czechoslovakia, Austria, Hungary as well as their metropoles Vienna, Prague, Budapest but also Warsaw, Berlin and Munich).

As an entity Central Europe disappeared after the Second World War. Countries which had accepted the Marshall Plan were geopolitically classified as belonging to the West whereas those which had rejected Marshall aid were absorbed into the Soviet bloc becoming part and parcel of Eastern Europe. The dividing line did not only run along the course of the Elbe between West and East Germany. Austria and Czechoslovakia, the two countries in the heart of Europe, had by force of political circumstances changed their quasi-geographical location: the former finding itself attached to the West and the latter to the East of Europe.

The substantial literature on Eastern Europe that has been published since the Cold War concentrated largely on the common aspects of the economies and societies of the countries designated as Eastern European. This created erroneously a monolithic picture which helped more plausibly to explain the domination of the Soviet Union over the territories between the Volga and the Elbe. However, just as the idea of *Mitteleuropa* of the first decades of the twentieth century is a myth, so is the concept of a monolithic post-1945 Eastern Europe a mythical construct.

It is the intention of this publication to approach the present transformation of Central and Southeast Europe soberly by striving to achieve a balance between common features and dissimilarities of the countries lying between Germany and Russia, but against the historical background of each of them. The contributions have been written by economists and economic historians who, like the editor, are deeply concerned with the prevalent ahistoricism in the assessments of the course of events since 1989. Through their differing approaches to their countries' twentieth century history, the contributors emphasize the considerable diversity within a region which has continuously been seen as more 'similar' than 'diverse'. Although the authors do not deny the presence of common features, at the same time, they identify clear differences arising from historical and cultural traditions, religions, nations and nationalities, political systems, social customs as well as levels of economic development. These significant dissimilarities have largely been disregarded in the West, just as they were ignored by the Soviets when they imposed their socio-economic system on their vassal states.

As the paths of post-1945 development are examined, analysed and discussed by the authors, they show that in spite of almost a half century of efforts of sovietization, deep-seated differences not only continued but also that individual Central and Southeast European countries reacted differently to similar circumstances. With respect to the post-1989 years there is a wide area of agreement amongst the authors that it is necessary to give a warning about the danger of replacing the failed Soviet 'model' by a no less schematic 'model' of free-market capitalism. Indeed, the authors substantiate their anxiety by examples of the failed introduction of such instant 'models' as, for instance in the cases of the former Yugoslavia (Štiblar), of East Germany (Roesler) and even of Poland (Szlajfer) where its success has generally but erroneously been taken for granted.

Although the emphasis in this volume is on economic questions, these are seen not only in terms of national income and growth rates, but are placed within a social and political setting. Much attention is devoted to the frequent dramatic upheavals and structural breaks in the countries' economic experience during the twentieth century. Průcha examines Czechoslovakia in terms of 'continuity with interruptions'. Why was interwar Austria convulsed by crisis after crisis? What was the basis of these frequent turning points? In surveying their history one can not but agree with Weber that the serious structural breaks that shook not only the Austrian economy but also every other country emanated from *political* causes.

While Austria's unique post-1945 position enabled her to reconstruct her economy by benefiting from Marshall aid and later to gain neutrality status, it also afforded her the luxury of neither following the Western nor the Eastern 'model'. Based on popular consensus, the leading parties in both government and in opposition learned the lessons of her crisis-ridden interwar history and of the years in the Third Reich following the *Anschluss*. This, as Weber so convincingly argues, facilitated the eventual success of Austria's sizeable mixed economy, which was established in the context of the Cold War. In neighbouring Czechoslovakia the lessons of her interwar as well as her post-1938 history loomed large after her liberation from Nazi occupation in 1945 in a rare popular consensus about establishing a fairer order of the economy in a democratic society. Yet her absorption into Eastern Europe brought about a complete change of direction ending in economic failure (Prûcha). The path of these two economically most advanced states of the region diverged and here they are considered in a comparative context.

When viewing in parallel the other countries of the former Eastern Europe, it becomes evident that the all pervading problem has been their mutual relative economic backwardness. Even in informed discussions of the transformation process taking place in the post-communist countries, the legacy of this economic backwardness is seldom fully appreciated. It is pointed out here that relative economic backwardness was a basic component of economic, social and political development. Poland and Romania - as Szlajfer and Daianu demonstrate - and also Hungary were unable either to overcome their backwardness or to rid themselves of dependency on the leading West European creditor nations during the interwar period (cf. Kaser). The war years were even less conducive to advance their industrialization for they brought domination, exploitation and destruction. Consequently the Soviet model of forced industrialization had a certain attractiveness and in the 1950s it produced a rush to industrial growth. In Hungary's case Ivan Berend (who regrettably was unable to contribute to this volume) characterizes this phase as 'obsolete modernization' which, after producing a spurt of economic growth, once more sucked the country back into relative backwardness. In Poland economic backwardness resulted not only in particular economic nationalism but in holistic economic nationalism. After adopting this the Soviet planning system led to mimetic industrialization and again exerted in time a wholly negative macro-economic effect (Szlajfer). When describing the Romanian efforts to overcome economic backwardness during the post-Second World War decades, Daianu characterizes their policy of import-substituting industrialization as immiserating growth.

It seems therefore essential that in the present process of transformation it should not be ignored that the roots of relative economic backwardness can already be found in the more distant past. Neither should the paradoxes of the present situation be ignored. These are pointed out by the authors: that a sober, scientific approach must recognize that the forty years of pre-1989 endeavours to overcome backwardness have turned agricultural into industrial societies, eliminated illiteracy and introduced universal free education from nursery school to universities. These are encouraging elements of a positive legacy for reconstruction.

The contributors to this volume raise relevant theoretical and practical questions, among them the relationship between 'market' and 'state'. Doubtless, the concept of the 'market economy' is used too vaguely and it is rarely realized that it is derived from Ludwig von Mises' philosophical understanding as part of the state in which the economy and society constitute a totality of the socio-economic order. In the widest sense it is the task of the state to prevent market failure and thus the new states need to perform this function by protecting the weak from the strong, to provide the necessary infrastructure as well as a financial system and a clearly defined legal order. These aspects are discussed in their historical and contemporary setting in this volume.

In conclusion I should like to thank Professor Philip L. Cottrell who has actively supported the idea of publishing the contributions to the Session on 'Eastern Europe' which I organized at the British Economic History conference (1992). The interceding years have given the authors a chance to verify their approach and to develop and substantiate their arguments. I wish to express my special gratitude to the Austrian Federal Ministry of Science and Research for creating favourable academic and scientific conditions in the framework of the research project 'The economic role of Austria in interwar Central Europe' under my direction.

March 1997

CHAPTER TWO

Eastern Europe in Transition: Economic Development during the Interwar and Postwar Period*

Alice Teichova

Preamble

The amazing, unexpected and rapid events that have occurred in Eastern Europe since November 1989 triggered major discussions in politics and economics both in East and West. Influential experts argue that, since communism, with its rigidly planned and centrally directed economic system, has failed, countries which had for the past forty years lived under it must immediately reverse into the capitalist system. The magic phrase of the post-communist governments is 'market economy' without qualifying it with adjectives such as 'social' or 'mixed' as the Finance Minister of Czechoslovakia, Václav Klaus, likes to repeat.[1] Does this mean the unfettered market of Adam Smith's capitalism of the 'invisible hand', which is a theoretical concept and in reality never really existed?[2] Another vexing question is why Western, but also domestic economic advisers of the newly elected governments of those countries, base their counsel on Thatcherism rooted in monetarism which has so obviously failed after a mere decade? Also the much debated 'shock treatment' prescribed for their ailing economies by eminent US experts, which led to distressing results in Latin-American countries, is unlikely to be the panacea they long for after their traumatic experiences in this century. Unfortunately, these coveted remedies are out of touch both with historical and contemporary realities.

Seen from a historical perspective one should not be too surprised about the drama of revolution and counter-revolution in Eastern European history. The new states, which after 1918 emerged from the break-up of four empires (the Ottoman, the Tsarist, the Wilhelmine and the Habsburg Empire), inherited a marked west to east gradient of relative economic backwardness (See Table 2.1). They had a long tradition of massive state intervention in their economies which continued throughout all political and social changes practically until the present time - except for interwar Czechoslovakia, although even in this case government controls were tighter than in similar democratic states with a capitalist market economy. Most importantly, when taking into account historical realities, none of the Central and Southeast European states - again except for interwar Czechoslovakia - have experienced a democratic system with a parliamentary form of government, i.e. a pluralistic political system which is held to be compatible with a functioning market economy.

Table 2.1 National income per head (in 1937 US $)

	1920	1929	1937
Czechoslovakia	115	181	170
Hungary	79	115	120
Poland	-	108	100
Romania	-	-	81
Yugoslavia	66	86	80
Bulgaria	-	60	75
United Kingdom	329	372	440
Germany	-	304	340
France	196	312	265

Source: E. Ehrlich, 'Infrastructure and an International Comparison of Relationships with Indicators of Development in Eastern Europe 1920-1950', *Papers in East European Economics*, no. 33 (August 1973).

Their historical experiences were marked by instability, crises and wars. Since 1918 the lives of the new states in this region have been traumatically affected by three great divides: the first in 1938/39 when, after two decades of formal political independence during which they endeavoured with no great success to build a viable capitalist economy, German destructive domination engulfed them; the second great change occurred after the Soviet Army broke the German military might in Eastern Europe in 1945 followed by a fundamental socio-economic transformation; and the third they are experiencing after the sudden collapse of the communist regimes in 1989.

I should like to contribute to a better understanding of past and present events by considering a few salient aspects of pre- and post-Second World War economic development in Central and Southeast Europe in historical context.

The interwar period
During the two decades between the two world wars the Central and Southeast European states were drawn more effectively into the international economy than before 1913 and thus they became closely involved in the competitive struggles of the great industrial powers.

In the first decade government policies were dominated essentially by the repercussions of the October Revolution of 1917 in Russia and the outcome of the First World War. They had to fit into the realities of the Versailles system as Central and Southeast Europe, formerly the main area of German but also of Austro-Hungarian influence, was included in the political, financial and capital spheres of interest of the *Entente* Powers.

The second decade of the interwar period was overwhelmingly shaped by the impact of the world economic crisis and the rise of fascism in Europe. The shock of the economic crisis followed by the mounting threat of the Third Reich set in motion the gradual disintegration of the political and economic structures which had determined economic policies in the 1920s and led to their complete breakdown after the Munich Agreement of 30 September 1938. Towards the end of the 1930s the competitive struggle between the Great Powers in the region was exacerbated as national socialist Germany directed its *Großraumwirtschaftspolitik* primarily towards the East of Europe.

As this broad outline of the interwar period represents an almost inexhaustible topic the following comments will be concentrated on three important aspects of the period before the Second World War which in 1945 again played a crucial role. The same aspects have once more emerged as the central problems of the Eastern European economies at the present time. They are concerned, in the first place, with land reforms, in the second place, with lack of capital, and, in the third place, with market problems.

Land reforms

The First World War had left a trail of devastation throughout Eastern Europe and had accentuated existing social problems, above all, land hunger, landlessness and pauperism which, in turn, had strengthened peasant political parties. Moreover, the Bolshevik Revolution in Russia had deeply influenced the peasants' urgent demand for redistribution of the land. These circumstances made land reforms inevitable, quite apart from the economic necessity of achieving greater efficiency in agricultural production as a vital background to industrialization. Thus the very first step taken by all new successor governments consisted of land reforms, which received legislative priority.

Since land reforms were introduced essentially as a political necessity arising out of the revolutionary years 1917 to 1919, they were not conceived primarily as a policy of modernization of agriculture. Therefore, except in Czechoslovakia, state policies connected with land reforms failed to stimulate technical improvements in order to increase agricultural productivity. In this context it has to be realized that throughout the interwar period agriculture remained technologically backward and the population dependent on the land in Southeast Europe amounted to 70-80 per cent, in Hungary and Poland between 55 and 65 per cent and only Czechoslovakia came nearer to West European occupational distribution with less than 30 per cent of the economically active population engaged in agriculture (See Table 2.2). Practically the whole region suffered from agricultural excess population.

Undoubtedly, social cause and effect of land reforms can be regarded as paramount - through them the structure of land ownership was changed in every country by state intervention, abolishing the last remnants of feudalism, and satisfying national sentiments by transferring landed property from alien to indigenous owners. The land reforms did succeed in preventing a revolution of the peasants, but they failed to overcome the scissors between agriculture and industry in the Central and Southeast European agrarian economies.

Table 2.2 Percentage distribution of the gainfully occupied population in six European countries

	Year	Agriculture & Fishing	Mining	Manufacture & handicraft	Commerce & transport	Admin., domestic service, etc.
1. Typically industrialized countries:						
Czechoslovakia	1930	28	2	40	14	16
2. Less industrialized countries:						
Hungary	1930	54	1	23	10	12
Poland	1931	65	1	16	8	10
3. Countries lagging in industrial development:						
Romania	1930	78	-	7	5	10
Yugoslavia	1931	79	-	11	4	6
Bulgaria	1934	80	-	8	4	8

Source: League of Nations, *Industrialization and Foreign Trade* (Geneva, 1945), pp. 26-7

Lack of capital and the problem of investment

As a result of the First World War the existing chronic deficiency in domestic capital supply deteriorated further at the same time as the demand for capital rose dramatically, not least because of rapidly rising postwar inflations. The small successor states found increasingly harsh conditions in their search for capital and they competed fiercely for credits and investments from the capital-exporting Western countries. Most immediately the East European governments endeavoured to prevent the socialization of industry which was demanded by the working population and which, in contemporary terms, meant the transfer of private ownership of large factories and big banks into the hands of the state. Notwithstanding revolutionary demands in all states under discussion here governments were successful in replacing socialization with nationalization by legally enforcing the transfer of foreign, former enemy-owned property - mainly in German and Austrian hands - wherever possible into domestic private ownership, preferably into the hands of the ethnic majority whose interests the state chiefly represented. This was realized by the purchase of shares in enterprises and banks from their foreign owners by the legal process known as *nostrification*. This instrument was primarily resorted to, in order to break the umbilical cord with Vienna in Central and Southeast Europe, and in Poland's case with Berlin.

It could not solve the capital shortage in the successor states because it did not at first produce new funds.

Under conditions of general capital shortage, however, not even the strongest domestic financial groups possessed sufficient resources to obtain majority holdings in leading industrial enterprises and banks. Thus foreign capital - manly from Western industrial and financial groups - was encouraged to participate in big business and large banks. Therefore, not only shifts in the distribution of ownership from foreign to domestic entrepreneurs but also from former enemy alien to contemporary friendly foreign investors took place. In this way new economic ties, above all, with London, Paris and New York, were forged.

While lack of capital remained a fundamental problem, Central and Southeast Europe constituted an important link in the chain of international economic relations and therefore capital export into this area was an integral part of the world-wide operations of Britain, France and the USA, which were politically, diplomatically and economically motivated. With regard to two aspects the *Entente* Powers essentially agreed. In the first place, Germany was to be eliminated as a serious trade partner; this included the prevention of renewed *Mitteleuropa* aspirations. In the second place, Central and Eastern Europe was to function as a barrier - a *cordon sanitaire* - against Soviet Russia.

It was also to serve as an alternative region for Western capital exports, in order to replace, at least partially, the losses suffered by British and French investors in Russia after the confiscation of foreign capital by the Soviet government.

Capital imports as direct participating investment contributed relatively most to capital accumulation but the foreign credits, which were requested with great urgency from the very inception of the successor states, had comparatively less positive effects on economic growth.

International investments reached their peak of the interwar period in 1930. With the onset of the economic crisis investment activity abated, but the distribution of long-term investment according to countries of origin remained essentially unchanged until the Munich Agreement of 1938. With regard to Central and Southeast Europe this meant that about 75 per cent of total foreign investment originated in Western Europe. Britain and France held either first or second place while Germany, which was leading before 1914, took up fifth place on the average (See tables 2.3 and 2.4). After 1929 contributions by foreign investors to domestic capital formation in the small states practically ceased, and from 1932 capital moved out absolutely from these countries. None of them was able to cover its outgoings with export surpluses, except Czechoslovakia. Although massive state intervention, particularly exchange controls and strict foreign trade regulation, did lead to export surpluses these proved insufficient fully to meet capital claims and commitments for interest and dividend payments (See table 2.5).

9

Table 2.3 Origin of foreign investments in joint-stock capital of Czechoslovakia, Poland, Bulgaria and Yugoslavia, 1937 (%)

Country of origin of foreign investment	Czechoslovakia (a)	Poland (b)	Bulgaria (c)	Yugoslavia (d)
Great Britain	30.8	5.5	1.1	17.3
France	21.4	27.1	9.2	27.5
Austria	13.1	3.5	-	-
Holland	8.8	3.5	0.4	2.1
Germany	7.2	13.8	9.3	6.2 (e)
Belgium	7.1	12.5	20.5	5.3
Switzerland	4.5	7.2	25.1	7.3
United States	3.5	19.2	11.1	12.0
Italy	2.2	-	13.2	3.1
Sweden	0.9	2.7	-	1.2
Hungary	0.5	-	2.3	2.0
Czechoslovakia	-	1.6	7.4	8.5
Other countries	-	3.4	0.4	-
Monaco				2.9
Poland				0.3
Liechtenstein				0.3
Luxemburg				0.5
Swiss Mixed Capital				2.6
Anglo-Dutch capital				0.8
US-French capital				0.1
Total	100.0	100.0	100.0	100.0

Notes: (a) Industry and banking; (b) Industry and trade; (c) All joint-stock companies in private enterprise; (d) Industry in private enterprise; (e) Includes Austria

Sources: Calculated from: Teichova, A. *An Economic Background to Munich, International Business and Czechoslovakia* (Cambridge, 1974), pp. 48-9; Wellisz, L. *Foreign Capital in Poland* (London, 1938), p. 151; Jurkovic, B. *Auslandskapital in Jugoslawien* (Berlin, 1941), p. 441; Aladjoff, P. 'Das Auslandskapital in Bulgarien' (dissertation, Berlin University, 1941), p. 55.

Under prevailing economic conditions in Central and Southeast European countries capital imports, especially foreign loans, had contributed very little to their economic development because - with the exception of Czechoslovakia - roughly more than three-quarters of the total foreign loans contracted in the interwar period were put either to cover budget deficits, consumption uses or prestige spending including excessive military expenditure, as well as to convert old debts repeatedly into new ones. Basically, the input of foreign capital was neither sufficient to generate economic growth nor did its presence provide a viable and secure home and export market for any of the countries. The result of procurement of foreign capital was that indebtedness rose, industrialization was slow and tariff walls grew ever higher.

Table 2.4 Comparative data on long-term foreign investment in six east-central and south-east European countries, 1937

	Foreign debt of government in % of total public debt	Direct foreign participation in industrial companies, banks and insurance companies, in % of total capital			
		Joint-stock companies	Limited companies	Banks	Insurance companies
Romania	89.2 (a)	83	-	75	70
Yugoslavia	82.5 (a)	61	-	75	52 (b)
Hungary	81.1 (a)	0.25	-	-	-
Bulgaria	72.3 (a)	48	-	31	30
Poland (1936)	63.0	44.2	89.7	29	65 (c)
Czechoslovakia (d)	17.5	29	3	15	26

Notes: (a) 1931-32; (b) 1936; (c) 1935; (d) Czechoslovakia was the only country in this area which also exported capital; - indicates date not known

Sources: Compiled from: Gross, H. *Südosteuropa, Bau und Entwicklung der Wirtschaft* (Leipzig, 1939); Berend, I.T. & Ránki, G. 'Capital Accumulation and the Participation of Foreign Capital in Hungarian Economy after the First World War', *Nouvelles Études Historiques* (1965); Jurković, B. *Auslandskapital in Jugoslawien* (Berlin 1941); Rozenberg, V. *Inostrani kapital v jugoslavenskoj privredi* (Belgrade, 1937); Aladjoff, P. 'Auslandskapital in Bulgarien' (dissertation, Berlin University, 1942. Teichova, A. *An economic background, op. cit.* L. Wellisz, *Foreign Capital in Poland* (London, 1938); *Annual Statistical Rômaniei* (1938, 39); *Statistischer Taschenbuch v. Rumänien* (1941).

Table 2.5 Discrepancy between debt service and income from foreign trade in six European countries 1931 (millions of Swiss francs)

	Amount of debt service for 1931	Total debt service as % of exports	Balance of trade
Austria	214	22	-622
Bulgaria	35	16	+47
Czechoslovakia	105	5	+213
Hungary	248	48	+16
Romania	203	28	+192
Yugoslavia	124	29	-15

Source: Ránki, G. *Economy and Foreign Policy: The Struggle of the Great Powers for Hegemony in the Danube Valley, 1919-1939* (New York, 1983), p. 121.

Market problems

In the wake of the financial crisis practically all capital imports dried up which exacerbated the chronic shortage of capital in Central and Southeastern European countries. Their economic problems could not be bridged by further credits; they could only begin to be solved by trying to achieve a favourable balance of trade by boosting exports and curbing imports. Consequently, as credits ceased, the search for markets became a priority at a time of a shrinking world market.[3] (See table 2.6)

Through the narrowing of foreign markets autarchic policies were enhanced by militant nationalism and dictatorial regimes in the region. Indeed, the comparatively free market economy of Czechoslovakia, the only remaining democratic state of a Western type in this area, was one of the hardest hit by the crisis and recovery was slower than in the predominantly agricultural economies (Cf.Figure 2.1)

Table 2.6 Size of trade decline during the crisis, 1933-38

	1933 as % of 1929		Maximum decline during crisis		1938 as % of 1929	
	Imports	Exports	Imports	Exports	Imports	Exports
Albania	58.7	40.4	68.3	70.8	59.5	66.7
Bulgaria	75.5	55.4	73.5	60.3	59.4	87.4
Czechoslovakia	71.0	71.5	72.8	71.5	38.1 (a)	40.7 (a)
Hungary	70.8	62.6	70.8	67.8	38.7	50.4
Poland	73.3	65.8	76.2	67.0	41.9	42.2
Romania	60.2	50.9	69.3	52.7	45.3	53.4
Yugoslavia	70.4	66.8	70.4	66.8	50.9	49.3
World	65.0	64.5	66.3	65.7	40.2	40.7
Europe	62.0	63.0	64.7	65.5	42.3	39.2

Note: (a) - January-September 1938

Source: Drábek, Z. 'Trade Performance of East European Countries 1919-1939', *Papers in East European Economics*, no. 37 (October 1973).

Intensified state intervention was to meet the problems of decreasing demand on the home market by cartel legislation, forced syndicalization and direct state entrepreneurship. Economic activity of the state was not seen as a temporary measure until things returned to 'normal' but became accepted practically and theoretically as a political necessity.

Where were the agrarian economies of Central and Southeast Europe to find markets for their main exports? Their chief creditors and investors (Britain, France and the USA) restricted access to their own home, colonial and dependent markets, and by their participation in industry and banking of the small economies they were indirectly extracting a share in the export-oriented business of these states. This represented a crucial handicap for the weaker Central and Southeast European economies, since the possibilities of paying their debts with commodity exports remained severely limited.

Germany embarked upon a policy of bilateral trade agreements with weaker Danubian countries who were attracted by her guarantees to purchase agrarian products they could not have sold elsewhere.[4] Bilateralism succeeded more immediately with Hungary and Yugoslavia, later with Bulgaria and Romania. With the advent of the Hitler government in 1933 and the implementation of the Schacht plan in 1934 the Danubian region was to be drawn more effectively into the German sphere of influence as part of the *Großraumwirtschaft*. As they traded increasingly with Germany they were piling up credit balances in *Sperrmark* at especially agreed rates of exchange because their exports to Germany on average exceeded their imports from Germany between 1930 and 1938. Bilateral trade with Germany did not aid industrialization of the less developed economies, nor engender a rising effective demand on their home markets, nor accelerate their economic growth to a remarkable extent as has been claimed. On the contrary, the larger Germany's share in Southeast European trade on a bilateral basis grew, the more the industrialization of the region was threatened. Indeed, it was the aim of national socialist policy to prevent indigenous industrialization as far as possible. Any limited economic growth in Eastern Europe which was attained in the 1930s was connected with their government's policy of import substitution.

The German *Großraumwirtschaftspolitik* solved its problems by force inflicting the loss of independence and enormous losses in lives and property on the peoples of Central and Eastern Europe.

The Second World War's horrific impact on Eastern Europe is a chapter of foreign domination, exploitation, mass murder and destruction.[5] Its exclusion from this contribution is only justified by the fact that the present objective is to assess and compare prewar with postwar economic development.

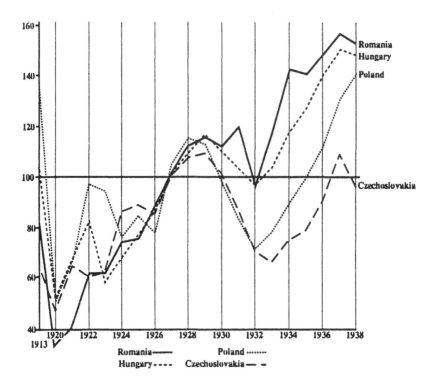

Figure 2.1 Annual manufacturing production in Romania, Hungary, Poland and Czechoslovakia, 1913-38

Source: Svennilson, *Growth and Stagnation in the European Economy* (Geneva, 1954), p. 207.

The post-1945 period

Just as the disappearance of Soviet influence in Eastern Europe is decisive in the changing situation at the present time, the decisive factor in postwar reconstruction of Eastern Europe was the dominant role played by the Soviet Union in this area. It was based on the historical reality that the Soviet Army had driven out the armed forces of National Socialist Germany. Soviet military presence was a political factor of paramount importance both in the former enemy states, i.e. allies of Germany (Romania, Bulgaria and Hungary) and in allied countries (Poland, Czechoslovakia and Yugoslavia). The intensity of Soviet ideological, political and economic pressures varied from country to country and in historical context one can observe a sliding scale from voluntary support, which was strongest in Tito's Yugoslavia until the break in 1948, and in Czechoslovakia where the KSČ (Communist Party of Czechoslovakia) became the leading party in free democratic elections in 1946, over the Soviet-friendly regime in Bulgaria, where there was a Russophile tradition, to strong enmity in Romania, Hungary and Poland. But in all countries the relief to be freed of German occupation engendered support for an alliance with the Soviet Union.

Except for Yugoslavia, where Soviet communism was adopted immediately, only to be abandoned three years later, the general type of communist regime developed in three stages following upon each other in quick succession between 1946 and 1948: the first stage was based on pluralism from centre to left, that is on coalitions of communists, social democrats, liberals and peasant parties; the second stage eliminated non-socialist groups from government, and during the third stage the so-called right-wing elements were purged from social democratic parties and the rest amalgamated with the communists thus obtaining a one-party communist rule. During the same period the policy of 'the specific way to socialism' adopted in each country after 1945 was abandoned in favour of the policy significantly hailed as 'the Soviet Union our example'.

As a result revolutionary socio-economic transformation took place which fundamentally changed the society and the economy in this region. In order to allow comparisons of the pre- and postwar economic development the following three main areas will be discussed: (1) agriculture, (2) industry, banking and investment, and (3) the economy and the introduction of central planning.

Land reforms

As in 1918 so in 1945 the demand for land reforms became the main political rallying point of peasants who were supported by the urban population and by the intelligentsia. Nationalism played a significant role because the land which was confiscated for redistribution had largely been taken over by Germans, Italians and collaborators. The result was curious as land was not nationalized (except for areas taken over by the state) but distributed to landless and small peasants. Thus the strata of small and middle peasants were greatly strengthened while large landowners were completely eliminated.

15

The land reforms of 1945 were radical but not in the sense of socialist nationalization. Only with the political decision to collectivize in the early 1950s - against all promises by the communist leaders *not* to do so - any efforts at building an efficient peasant agriculture ceased. The ensuing exodus from countryside to towns left agriculture with a dwindling and over-aged workforce and, as investment was deliberately curtailed by the planners, productivity fell. Thus agriculture badly lagged behind all other sectors of the economy. The only collectivized agriculture which succeeded in Eastern Europe - but effectively only as late as the 1970s and 1980s - was that of Czechoslovakia. But this was a Pyrrhic victory if we consider the whole economic development. In this framework the agricultural sector failed in all countries of Eastern Europe.

Industry, banking and investment
The immediate post-war situation was extraordinarily favourable to nationalization of the big banks and large industrial enterprises: German ownership acquired by aggression and war was liquidated, the property of indigenous capitalists who had collaborated with the Germans was confiscated, Jewish ownership lapsed as these entrepreneurs and bankers had perished in concentration camps and some had emigrated and did not return. In this way the most important industrial and financial assets were automatically transferred into state ownership. In Poland and Yugoslavia these assets comprised two thirds of total industrial capacity.

Next to land reforms the most popular demand was the nationalization of large industry and banks. This accelerated the nationalization legislation everywhere in Eastern Europe. Between 1945 and 1949 over 90 per cent of industrial capacity was nationalized. Finance and banking was entirely taken over by the governments. In this expropriation without compensation the economic basis of the middleclass was destroyed after 1949 and this was followed by the dissolution of the economic stronghold of tradesmen and shopkeepers, that is the lower middle-class. All entrepreneurial functions were transferred to planners.

The path to the centrally planned economies of Eastern Europe
No assessment of the last forty years can be made without considering the objectives and functioning of economic planning.

After the end of the Second World War there was no serious opposition to economic planning. On the contrary, there was a widespread belief in the necessity of socialist reforms and in the need for economic planning to avoid repetition of the harsh economic crisis of the 1930s which had led to fascism and war. There existed a clear preference for a more just and egalitarian society and for an economic democracy based on planning. These aspects were still recognizable in the first short-term plans for reconstruction between 1946 and 1948. However, communists in the individual governments used this support to strengthen their positions and force through one-party Soviet type regimes within a short period of time.

Thus planning was not imposed against opposition in the first instance since there existed favourable preconditions for its realization: historically there was a long tradition of state intervention in Eastern Europe; immediately, there existed a situation of postwar scarcity which demanded the control of production, distribution and consumption; ideologically, a broad consensus among economists, sociologists and political philosophers considered socialist planning as the best method to overcome backwardness - controversies did not question the necessity for planning but were concerned with different views about objectives and methodology of economic plans. Debates about approaches to economic planning were stopped by the communist take-over during 1948 and 1949 after the rejection of the Marshall Plan by East European states and the division of Europe which created the two Germanies and led to the founding of NATO, the Council for Mutual Economic Assistance (CMEA) and the Warsaw Pact.

By February 1949 all initiatives in the direction of economic democracy including the pluralistic concept of central planning had been suppressed and the hierarchical structure of centrally administered and directed economies became an imitation of the Soviet system, disregarding differences in cultural traditions and social and economic levels. The system was mechanically transplanted from the USSR to Eastern Europe except for Yugoslavia. The basis as well as objectives of all economic theory and planning became the maximization of economic growth through the greatest increase in production - the five year plans developed against this background.

At the same time the CMEA was to advance the economic integration of its member states. Yet, instead of a division of labour and integration, autarchic tendencies became dominant. Co-operation was essentially limited to trade relations which were turned round from west to east and the whole trade network was brought into the realm of trade with the Soviet Union, the so-called 'radial' pattern (70 per cent of each country's trade tied to the USSR).

High-pressure industrialization and armament production strained the economies of Eastern Europe, especially Czechoslovakia's, to breaking point. Targets of the first five year plan in each country were unrealistically increased, heavy industry absorbed labour and resources to the detriment of agriculture and particularly of consumer goods industries. This policy became known as 'the iron concept', also as the basis of Stalinism. Investments were pumped into producer goods while funds for consumer goods and service industries were cut back to such an extent that demand greatly exceeded supply. Retail trade and small-scale industry were brought under state direction and administration. When this happened, the price system was entirely separated from demand and supply. It served fully as an instrument of central planning. The economy developed into a state controlled seller's market.

In the first years of economic planning this led to an unparalleled rate of economic growth (11 to 16 per cent between 1949 and the mid-1950s). This was regarded by the communist parties and their governments (with a proliferating bureaucratic apparatus) as evidence of success. The policy 'the

Soviet Union our example' seemed to confirm the infallibility of the Soviet leadership and the communist parties, and the possibility of achieving socialism and communism in a very short space of time. However, it was not long before the policy of *maximum* growth instead of *optimum* growth began to manifest itself in negative consequences. As the incidences of bottlenecks and failures increased, they were linked to so-called activities of 'enemies of the state, traitors and spies'. At the height of Stalinism this led to show trials in which numerous people were sentenced to death or long-term imprisonment under the slogan 'the enemy in our ranks'. Although this scapegoat policy spread fear and put populations under political pressure, it was unable to reverse the consequences of misdirected planning.

What were the consequences? The original aims of economic planning, which were to lead to continuously rising living standards and more democracy in production and consumption decisions, had been sacrificed to the fundamentally erroneous assumption made by planners that a continuous increase in gross capital investment and in output of producer goods is the hallmark of an efficient economy. Already the third five year plans could not meet their targets and had to be abandoned. The centrally planned and administered economy was not capable of co-ordinating the processes of economic life. This was reflected in the economic crisis of the early 1960s which showed declining, indeed negative growth rates. The system slithered into crises which were held to be impossible in a socialist economy.

But the planned economies, by relying mainly on extensive rather than intensive growth, had run up against barriers of growth where every increase in production, in the rule, required a higher level of investment than in the past. The mounting pressure for reforms became evident but the basic dilemma of the planners to combine perceptible improvements of living standards with continuous economic expansion remained unresolved because, with the exception of the brief period of the reform movement of the 1960s, especially in Czechoslovakia, the priorities of central planners remained 'economic growth' based on continuous increases in investment, as well as greater output of producer goods and higher defence expenditures. Therefore, the problems repeated themselves in the long run, albeit with varying degrees of severity.

Among the greatest obstacles to reform was, above all, the magnitude of the party apparatus which could only have been reduced by eliminating the dual subordination system whereby the party apparatus had the right of supervision and interference at every level of the economic structure. In addition the communist leadership feared that the political cohesion of the Soviet bloc could become unstuck by devolution of economic decision making and the introduction of - even a regulated - market mechanism. The party elite was neither prepared to permit workers, co-management nor to tolerate greater democratic freedoms. This gives a certain idea of the political significance of the tenacious resistance of the ruling elites to economic reforms.

Economic reform in most East European countries had really never been given a chance. The last effective chance was lost when the comprehensive economic, social and political reforms were stopped by military action of the Warsaw Pact led by the Soviet Union during the 'Prague Spring' of 1968.

There existed a groundswell of reform movements which grew from the later 1950s, was stifled during the 1970s, but could not be kept down during the 1980s. Most consistently, though under constraints, reforms were pursued peacefully in Hungary, most persistently, accompanied by violent clashes, reforms were demanded in Poland, and most timidly, by drawing up secret plans, reforms were prepared in Czechoslovakia. But in none of these countries were communist governments prepared to reform and democratize the economic and political system simultaneously. From this historical view the changes of 1989 do not seem so surprising, except for their suddenness and the speed of the collapse of communism which had held sway over Eastern Europe for forty years.

Conclusion

To return to the introduction. One has to be cautious about prompt explanations for the demise of the Soviet-type system and about offers of instant remedies for the economic plight of the populations of the Eastern European countries, which have not been lacking since 1989. Here it suffices to mention only three such judgements arising from the upheavals in Eastern Europe: the changes were hailed as 'The victory of the enterprise culture' by the followers of Thatcherism, while members of the Adam Smith Institute saw them as 'The triumph of Western capitalism', and in Fukujama's view of the contemporary world they seemed to confirm the dawning of 'The end of history'.

All these appraisals seem somewhat premature in the light of recent developments both in the West and in the East. Serious judgements about the spectacular failure of the communist regimes can be arrived at only after thoroughly analysing the social and economic realities in Eastern Europe in historical context. It is the author's belief that on the basis of such analyses it is possible to draw conclusions about socio-economic policies for the reconstruction of the societies and economies of these countries. 'Shock treatment' alone is bound to do more harm than good, for in the countries of Eastern Europe the legal system has no provision for relieving hardships arising from an uninhibited market economy.

In this connection it is perhaps significant to quote in conclusion from Václav Havel's sombre message on the first anniversary of the 'velvet revolution':

> Today we are standing here rather embarrassed. We know very well what we have to accomplish. Why do we find it so difficult to launch our joint project off the ground? Dissatisfaction, nervousness, insecurity and disillusionment are widespread in our society ... rancour, rivalry, mutual denigration, envy and boundless ambition is infecting public life.[6]

Notes

* A draft of this paper was first presented at the University of Umeå on 27 November 1990 on the occasion of the University's 25th Anniversary Celebrations. It was extended and rewritten during my Fellowship at the Centre for Humanities at Oregon State University, Corvallis, USA, where I gave a lecture on the topic of the paper. It was presented at the Annual Conference of the British Economic History Society in Leicester (10-12 April 1992). For the collegiate atmosphere and favourable working conditions I wish to express my thanks to Peter Copek, the Director of the Centre for the Humanities. The paper draws largely from two research projects supported by the Economic and Social Research Council (UK) for which I wish to express my thanks. In the first project on the 'Economic History of Eastern Europe' I participated in a research team under the direction of Michael C. Kaser which resulted in the publication of Kaser, M.C. & Radice, E.A. (eds), (1985), *The Economic History of Eastern Europe 1919-1975*, vol. I, *Economic Structure and Performance between the Two Wars*, vol. II. Oxford, (1986), *Interwar Policy, the War and Reconstruction*. Oxford; and Kaser, M.C. (ed.), (1986), *Institutional Change within a Planned Economy*, vol. III. Oxford. The second research project on 'Multinational companies in interwar East-Central Europe', which I directed, resulted in the publication of Teichova, A. & Cottrell, P.L. (eds), (1983), *International Business and Central Europe 1919-1939*. Leicester and New York. I am also grateful to Cambridge University Press for the permission to use my publication (1974), *An economic background to Munich International Business and Czechoslovakia 1918-1938*. Cambridge; and my contribution to Mathias, P. & Pollard, S. (eds), (1989), *The Cambridge Economic History of Europe*, vol. VIII, chapter XIII 'East-central and south-east Europe 1919-1939', pp. 887-983. Cambridge. In addition I drew from my book (1988), *Kleinstaaten im Spannungsfeld der Großmächte. Wirtschaft und Politik in Mittel- und Südosteuropa in der Zwischenkriegszeit*. Vienna, Munich

1 On the policy of the Czechoslovak Finance Minister, cf. 'Václav Klaus předseda OF' ('Václav Klaus Chairman of OF' [OF=Občanské Forum = Civic Forum]) *Hospodářské noviny*, 15.10.90; cf. also Barrett, R. & Green, P. 'Can Czechoslovakia rediscover its enterprise?' *The Times. The Next Frontier. A Business Guide to Central and Eastern Europe*, 6.11.1990, p. 12.

2 Such attitudes are irrational and anachronistic and seem to be rather a sign of helplessness in face of the economic realities in Eastern Europe. Indeed, the Western capitalist economy of the twentieth century, so coveted by the new Eastern European governments, in contrast to the

'free' market economy of the nineteenth century, is widely held to be 'managerial capitalism' regulated by 'the visible hand' of managers. Cf. Chandler, A.D. Jr. (1977), *The Visible Hand. The Managerial Revolution in American Business*. Cambridge, Mass.

3   György Ránki examines the economic and political implications of the limited policy choices of Southeast European states between credit and market in his book, (1983), *Economy and Foreign Policy. The Struggle of the Great Powers for Hegemony in the Danube Valley 1919-1939*. New York.

4   I return to this question in my essay in memory of my dear friend György Ránki, 'Bilateral trade revisited: Did the Southeast European states exploit national socialist Germany on the eve of the Second World War?', in Glatz, F. (ed.), (1990), *Modern Age - Modern Historian in Memoriam György Ránki (1930-1988)*. Budapest, pp. 193-209.

5   The so far most detailed analysis of the economic impact of the Second World War in Eastern Europe is to be found in Kaser & Radice (eds), *op. cit.*, vol. II, chapters 13 to 19, pp. 299-492.

6   Quoted by Green, P. 'Bush visit disappoints Czechs', *The Times*, 19.11.1990.

CHAPTER THREE

Continuity and Discontinuity in the Economic Development of Czechoslovakia, 1918-91

Václav Průcha

1. Interwar period

Long periods of continuity in economic development of different countries are usually interrupted by periods of prevailing discontinuity or periods characterized by at least some distinct features of discontinuity. Discontinuity is typical of periods of formation or disintegration of states, periods of wars, social revolutions or other upheavals. Of course, some features of the economy (e.g. structure of industrial sectors, territorial location of industries) cannot be immediately altered, although there are always efforts to hasten the transformation.

Since its birth in 1918, Czechoslovakia has suffered more frequent interruptions of continuous historical development, and most of the interruptions have been more severe than in the economically advanced countries in Western Europe and overseas. Seven turning points with distinct features of discontinuity can be traced within the 74-year period of Czechoslovakia's existence: these include the separation of the new state from the former Austro-Hungarian Monarchy; the destruction of the state in 1938-39 and its integration in the Nazi 'large space economy' (*Großraumwirtschaft*); renewal of the state and the revolutionary changes of 1945-48; the implanting of the Soviet system of management and control; restructuring, new territorial orientation of foreign trade and socialization of the economy early in the Cold War period; the attempt to reform the society and economy in 1968, followed by 'normalization' based on the Brezhnev doctrine; and finally, the attempt to re-establish a market economy which started in 1990 and which is still far from finished.

The disintegration of the Austro-Hungarian Monarchy after the First World War was associated with a disintegration of the economies of the successor states. The new Czech and Slovak leaders did their best to achieve, as soon and as widely as possible, a full political and economic detachment from Vienna and Budapest: there were worries that continuity of economic ties would lead to attempts to re-establish, in another form, the Austro-Hungarian Empire.

The economic separation from Austria and Hungary was effected through the separation of currencies, associated with a policy of deflation; the new state supported the transfer of stock ownership to Czech, Slovak and West-European shareholders, declared a land reform to take land from the aristocracy committed to the previous regime, and tried to replace Vienna's initial role in the re-export of Czechoslovak goods by direct trade contacts: new markets were sought to push the focus of trade from Austria and Germany to other territories. The industrial structure policy was also driven by efforts to overcome the Austrian inheritance. On the other hand, the economic policy of the Czechoslovak Government supported the integration of the western and eastern parts of the country whose mutual contacts had been poor before 1918.

During the time of political liability, economic chaos and startling hyperinflation in the countries around Czechoslovakia, the energetic approach of the Czechoslovak government to economic policy met a favourable response in the *Entente* countries. Czechoslovakia was considered as an island of stability in Central Europe and won international credit. Business circles in *Entente* countries began to draw distinctions between development in Czechoslovakia and other Central European countries: they exported capital to Czechoslovakia and later bought Czechoslovak crowns *en masse*, hoping to make a fortune from the revaluation of the Czechoslovak currency.

After 1918, discontinuity manifested itself in Czechoslovakia in the areas of internal and foreign policy, in culture, in the nationality policy, and, in the Czech Lands, even in the area of religion - people left the Catholic Church in droves. Several reforms were also made in social policy: new laws in that area were much more advanced than the welfare laws before the war. Discontinuity in the economy was characterized, in addition to the factors mentioned above, by changes in banking to the detriment of the big Vienna banking institutions, and in the structure of exporters of capital to Czechoslovakia.

However, discontinuity can hardly be traced in the structure of the economy: the industry of the new state maintained the inherited sectorial structure with an excess proportion of light and food industries (until 1929), whereas the proportion of processing sectors of heavy industries and the volume of power generation were poorer than in the majority of advanced countries. The causes of the delay in overcoming this unfavourable structure included, among others, the good and rapid development of industrial production in the 1920s, exerting only slight pressure on the necessity to restructure. Some light industry sectors exported 80 or 95 per cent of their output and were very vulnerable to any change in external demand. The territorial distribution of industries was affected by the fact that many factories in Slovakia, whose industrialization was generally poor, were closed down as a result of the disintegration of the Austro-Hungarian Monarchy: some of these plants were moved by their owners to Hungary, others failed to compete with the more advanced Czech industrial companies.

The disintegration of the Monarchy caused psychological depression in Austria and Hungary, and many contemporary local and foreign business experts believed that those countries' economic futures would be grim. On the other hand, in Czechoslovakia, which had the strongest economy of all the successor states, independence acted as a psychological stimulus to new business development.

International statistics show that until 1929 economic development in Czechoslovakia was stronger than in Austria. According to *European Historical Statistics 1750-1970* by B.R. Mitchell, the 1929 gross national product exceeded that of 1913 by 52 per cent in Czechoslovakia, but only by 5 per cent in Austria, the average level for 1920-29 being 19 per cent higher than in 1913 in Czechoslovakia and 11 per cent lower in Austria.[1] The index for processing industries in 1929 was higher in Czechoslovakia than on an average for eighteen European countries, better values being recorded only in Greece, Finland, the Netherlands and Italy. The index in Czechoslovakia, perhaps slightly overrated, stood at 172 points (1913=100); in Austria it was 118 points and in Hungary 114 points.[2] As to the volume of exports, Austria was slightly above Czechoslovakia but on the other hand, the balance of Czechoslovak foreign trade regularly showed surpluses whereas in Austria - also regularly - it showed high deficits.[3]

After 1923 Czechoslovakia succeeded in increasing the population's standard of living compared with that before the war. But even earlier, from 1918, an eight-hour work day, state support in unemployment and protection of tenants were guaranteed by law and citizens enjoyed wide civic rights. Several hundreds of thousands of peasants were given land by land reform legislation. Old-age and invalid pensions for workers were introduced in 1924. Real wages and personal consumption continuously grew until 1929.

An answer to the question of how the disintegration of the Monarchy influenced economic development in its former territory would require a generalized overview free of any patriotic bias. The data would vary between countries and there would even be differences between regions within each country. The positive figures characterizing developments in Czechoslovakia until 1929 suggest that from the Czechoslovak point of view, this first discontinuity had largely positive consequences. Perhaps even the narrowing of the internal market after the collapse of the Monarchy had, in addition to its adverse effects, one favourable feature: it forced producers and traders to apply much initiative to improve quality, to innovate in their product range and to reduce costs. It is also important to note that the disintegration of the Monarchy stopped the flow of capital to the former Monarchy's centres (or at least reduced this flow in companies in which Austrian or Hungarian capital was still involved).

The economic crisis of the 1930s was profound and lengthy in Czechoslovakia. This statement is corroborated by a number of data. In 1929-33 Czechoslovak industrial output dropped by 40 per cent, the capacity of goods traffic decreased by almost one-half, and foreign trade turnover in terms of current prices dropped by more than 70 per cent. The number of unemployed in Czechoslovakia, a country with a population of less than fifteen million, reached one million.[4] From the point of view of industrial production, the world crisis culminated in the year 1932; in Czechoslovakia, however, it peaked one year later.

A number of facts can be put forward to explain this extraordinary depth and length of the crisis. The struggle between various groups of capital gave rise to a confused economic policy which did not correspond to the objective needs of the country and reacted too late to the situation. Though it was vitally important for the country's economy to promote exports, the tariff policy of the late 1920s was characterized by hard protectionism which had been enforced by the influential group of agrarian capital. The counter-measures of trade partners abroad undermined the export opportunities of Czechoslovak industry, which manifested itself most clearly in the difficulties experienced by Czechoslovak exporters to countries of Southeastern Europe.

Czechoslovak exporting capacity was further impaired by the monetary policy of adhering to a high exchange rate, fixed to gold in 1929, i.e. shortly before the onset of the crisis. The first devaluation of the Czechoslovak crown was enacted as late as 1934, much later than in many other countries. The high rate of exchange of the Czechoslovak crown weakened the competitiveness of Czechoslovak products abroad and stimulated imports, thus increasing the tension in the balance of payments. In addition, the competitiveness of a number of products was based on fairly low wages, which depressed demand in the home market and protracted the crisis. The end of the crisis was also delayed by drastic cuts in the incomes of farmers - this was linked to the onset of the agrarian crisis in 1928. Though the interrelationship between agrarian and industrial crises was characteristic of many countries, Czechoslovak agriculture continued playing an important part in the economy, being much more market-oriented than, say, agriculture in the Balkan countries.

The unfavourable development of the Czechoslovak economy in the 1930s may also have been due to limited state intervention in the economy. Although the interventions intensified in comparison with the 1920s, they remained below the level of such measures in most other countries.

But, according to Czechoslovak economic historians, the main cause of the extremely unfavourable development of the economy in the 1930s must be sought in the outdated structure of industrial production. The cyclical crisis of 1929-33 was, in Czechoslovakia, also a structural crisis of its industrial production and exports. In the 1930s, Czechoslovakia started to overcome the obsolete Austro-Hungarian pattern of its economy and a new, modern structure of industrial sectors began to take shape. However, this process took place under conditions of a reduced volume of aggregate industrial production. The state authorities failed to control the process so that development remained more or less spontaneous, involving immense economic losses, bankruptcies of thousands of manufacturing and craft businesses, keen competition between various groups of capital, mass unemployment, impoverishment of large regions of the country and unprecedented acuteness of social, political and nationalist conflicts. The situation was aggravated by the multinational pattern of the population as well as by the aggressive policy of Nazi Germany.

The economic decline of the 1930s had long-lasting effects upon the views and ideas within Czech and Slovak society. The generation entering its productive age in the later 1920s and early 1930s had an opportunity to learn the capitalist system in its most distorted forms - a destructive crisis and then a fascist war economy. Bitter disappointment came with the decision of the four Powers in Munich, (30 September 1938) by which Czechoslovakia was left to the tender mercies of Germany; the long-continued foreign-policy orientation pursued by Presidents T.G. Masaryk and E. Beneš was ruined. The Slovak nation demanded, rightfully, the recognition of its national sovereignty and a guarantee of its economic, social and cultural advancement. The achievements of the first five year plans in the Soviet Union raised much interest and great hopes.

Although an overwhelming part of the German minority fell for the ideology of Nazism, there was an increasingly marked political shift to the left, manifesting itself in the period starting with the 1930s and ending after the Second World War, first in the Czech Lands, later in Slovakia. These changes in society's mind motivated a revolutionary process which, in turn, gave rise to the national democratic revolution in 1944–45.

2. The Second World War and revolutionary changes 1945-48

In the autumn of 1938 and in mid March 1939, Czechoslovakia fell victim to the aggressive policy of fascist regimes. The country was cut into five parts. After seizure of the border regions by Germany, Hungary and Poland, the German Army occupied the remaining parts of the Czech Lands and established the Protectorate of Bohemia and Moravia. Slovakia, deprived of its most fertile land in the south (seized by Hungary), became a puppet state, fully dependent on Germany. The Carpatho-Ukraine was annexed to Hungary.

The consequences of the four Powers' agreement in Munich included Czechoslovakia's falling within the area of interest of Nazi Germany. This led to a political and economic disintegration of the country; the reduction of economic contacts between the Protectorate and the Slovak state - and the southern part of Slovakia seized by Hungary and the Slovak state - was a marked feature of economic disintegration. On the other hand, economic tools and political as well as military pressure were used to integrate parts of the former state into the *Grossraumwirtschaft*, built by the Nazis. The Czech Lands were regarded as part of Greater Germany which was to have been the industrial core of Hitler's 'New Europe'. Slovakia, on the other hand, was considered as a supplier of foodstuffs and raw materials.

The events of 1938-39 were conducive in Czechoslovakia, among other things, to a discontinuity in economic development. This discontinuity was more pronounced in the Protectorate and the border areas of the Czech Lands compared with Slovakia. There is ample evidence to support this view. The controlled war economy (*gelenkte Wirtschaft*) altered the whole mechanism of the economy in which the state played a strong part. Large changes were also made in the social area (forced labour, regulation of workforce movement, regulation of wages and prices, the rationing system of supplies to the population). Militarization of the economy suppressed the manufacture of 'civil' products and resulted in an unprecedented extension of the production of goods important for the war. Also, many plants in former Czechoslovakia produced parts which were then assembled elsewhere.

In the Protectorate the militarization of industry destroyed a large number of small Czech businesses, from where the workers were transferred to the arms industry or to industrial establishments in Germany.

Germanization of the economy, also including aryanization (transfer of Jewish property to German hands), was a manifestation of discontinuity in the ownership structure. Long-continued development was also broken in a number of other areas - in the use of many methods of exploitation of the Czechoslovak economy, in the re-orientation of external economic relations, in a change in the structure of crop production and export, in the inflationary development of the currency and (in the Protectorate) in forceful interventions in the social structure of the population (oppression and reduction of the social group of creative intelligentsia, Germanization of the leading posts of state administration and companies, 'screening' of small businesses, closing of universities, reduction of secondary and technical schools, loss of qualifications in large groups of workers, especially in light industries). Other serious features of discontinuity were, in March 1939, the introduction of the German Mark in addition to the Crown in circulation in the Protectorate, and the abolition of customs barriers between the Protectorate and Germany in 1940.

In Slovakia the features of discontinuity were less distinct. War control of the economy was introduced later and was not so thorough as in the Protectorate. As Slovak industry was weak, militarization did not interfere with light industries: it manifested itself merely in successive changes in production structure with a differentiated rate of growth in the different industrial sectors. Germanization of the economy was less intensive. Jewish property seized from its owners was transferred to Slovak aryanizers. Unlike in the Protectorate, the middle and upper classes of society in Slovakia were economically strengthened during the first years of the war. However, the clerico-fascist regime of the Slovak state soon fell into isolation and the Slovak National Rising, which broke out in a large part of Slovak territory in August 1944, declared requirements which later constituted a basis for revolutionary changes in the whole country.

The idea of continuity of social order with the interwar period was dismissed during the final stage of the Second World War. Radical interventions in the economy were required, in addition to changes in political structure and in the structure and relations of the nationalities. The results of the free elections in 1946 were a victory for the left-oriented forces.[5] Socialist orientation was very strong (stronger in the Czech Lands than in Slovakia), though there were large differences in what different people understood as socialism: the leftists, including some members of the Communist Party, believed that Czechoslovakia should seek its own way towards socialism, and that socialism should be associated with political and economic plurality; large ownership of capital was expected to be reduced.

The Soviet Union seemed to respect the different countries' specific paths towards socialism in Central and Southeastern Europe until the middle of 1947. This can be supported by Stalin's statements of that time and by the fact that all Soviet troops were withdrawn from Czechoslovakia during 1945.[6] It was before the rift with Yugoslavia that a change in the Soviet standpoint was revealed in July 1947 by the pressure exerted upon the Czechoslovak government to refuse the Marshall Plan.

Large changes were made in the Czechoslovak economy during 1945-47. The seizure of the property of those who betrayed the nation and collaborated with the Nazis, far-reaching land reforms and the nationalization (in October 1945) of large industries, banks and insurance companies were, until 1989, the largest change in ownership structure in the modern history of the country. The public sector became the focus of the economy, though there was also some extension in the small-scale private production base (mainly in agriculture) and partly in private trade. At the same time, large estates were reduced and scope for capitalist enterprise was generally narrowed.

The controlled economy, taken over from the occupation period, successively changed into a system of national economic planning. A two-year plan was introduced in January 1947: its main purpose was to finish the postwar renewal of the economy. The two-year plan did not have a directive nature and still used economic tools to guide enterprises in making the desired decisions. It did not include substantial changes in the structure of the economy, except in regional policy, in which it became a starting point for a long-lasting process of industrialization of the economically underdeveloped parts of the country, especially Slovakia.

The first postwar years saw unprecedented migration of the population. About 800,000 people returned from forced labour in Germany, from prisons and concentration camps and from political emigration. Another 150,000 Czechs and Slovaks moved back from foreign countries where they had been living before 1938. The transfer of Germans from Czechoslovakia, effected upon the decision of the Allies, affected three million people (including German anti-fascists who where allowed to stay in Czechoslovakia , but most of whom decided to go to the Soviet zone of Germany). On the other hand, Czech citizens who had been expelled by the Germans in 1938-39 now returned to the border regions and were accompanied by hundreds of thousands of new settlers. The migration of 1945-47 involved, in total, about 5.5 million people.[7]

Before Czechoslovakia could fully recover from the war and re-establish a market economy, serious internal and international political events decided the country's fate. The later 1940s saw a destruction of the hope of a longer continuity of development which would have been based on a stabilization of postwar social changes.

3. Transition to a highly-centralized directive management system and the attempt to change it in 1968

Late in the 1940s the economic policy of Czechoslovakia was determined by several factors: the seizure of power by the Communist Party in February 1948 and the subsequent establishment of the 'general line of the construction of socialism' in the spring of 1949, the abandonment of the specifically Czechoslovakian route to socialism, increasing dependence on the Soviet Union, and by the introduction of Soviet methods into all areas of the society and economy. Within the East-West relationship, the disintegration of the Allies' coalition led to the Cold War. Czechoslovakia, 80 per cent of whose foreign trade was with Western countries in 1946-47 (the share of the USSR was 7 per cent)[8] was now hit by trade embargoes and by other forms of economic discrimination.

These intrinsic factors, combined with Czechoslovakia's own political decisions, greatly affected economic policy in Czechoslovakia after 1948. Economic policy was characterized by a whole complex of interconnected goals: application of the Soviet management and economic planning system associated with the abandonment of the principles of the market economy; destruction of the capitalist sector; accelerated socialization of agriculture and small private businesses in the economy; maximization of economic growth rates; restructuring of the economy with emphasis on the development of heavy industry; industrialization of Slovakia as part of an effort to equalize the standards of living in the eastern and western parts of the country; successive shifts of focus in external economic relations to CMEA countries; shifts in the commodity structure of exports from consumer goods to engineering products; achievement of economic independence from the West and strengthening of defence capability.

An especially important and still frequently disputed question is the structural policy in the period of the first five-year plan (1949-53). The original five-year plan of 1948 envisaged changes in the pattern of industry that were in line with the expected future needs of the Czechoslovak economy. Heavy industry was to grow faster than consumer-based industries, but the divergence of the planned growth rates was not extreme. The planned production increments were realistic and so were the anticipated increasing living standards.

The growth of international tension and the foreign pressure exerted on Czechoslovakia's economy led in 1950 and more noticeably in 1951 to a substantial increase and restructuring of the planned tasks included in the original five-year plan: thus it underwent a large qualitative change. The priority of selected heavy industries was underlined, mainly iron ore extraction, iron and steel production and non-ferrous metallurgy, as well as heavy and precision engineering. Considerable amounts of capital were devoted to geological prospecting. Additional production tasks connected with the strengthening of defence capability of the countries of the Soviet bloc were set up outside the framework of the five-year plan.

The adjustments of the plan speeded up the construction and restructuring of industry, but a considerable proportion of the priorities were shifted towards branches which, though currently representing bottlenecks in the whole socialist community, could not be efficient for Czechoslovakia in the long run. A highly fuel-, energy-, and material-intensive industrial pattern was established; it still survives. Some targets set in 1950-51 proved to be unrealistic and had to be scaled down in 1953. The huge extent of capital investment and the growth of defence outlays constrained resources available for the improvement of living standards, which stagnated in 1951-53.[9]

In the course of the first five-year plan period, a transition was under way, culminating in 1953, towards a highly centralized directive management system of the economy which was applied in Czechoslovakia according to the then prevailing Soviet system.

Planning became more comprehensive, detailed and binding, and embraced all segments of the economy. The plans now had a mobilizing nature and were much tighter. Directive allocation of tasks to enteprises in one-year plans served as an implementative tool. Enterprises had to meet not only production plans, but also plans dealing with supplies to the internal and to the export market, cost reduction, labour, wages, productivity, credit etc. Gross output became a major planning indicator: plans for labour productivity, remuneration funds and bonuses were derived from the gross output indicator. Market relations between enterprises receded into the background and were replaced by detailed central control of material and technical supplies.

The changes in the system of management early in the 1950s are difficult to appraise. Evaluating the objectives of economic policy and conditions in the climate of the Cold War, it must be admitted that centralization of resources and the directive nature of management were necessary. However, the interventions went far beyond an optimum level and extent. The central authorities were overwhelmed by operative problems, initiatives by enterprises were broken, and controversies between the enterprises and central authorities during the bargaining about the plans reappeared every year. The administrative methods of pricing, with no reference to market conditions, made it impossible to take rational decisions. Enterprises concealed their reserves and exaggerated their demand for raw materials, capital investments and labour resources.

The weaknesses of this administrative system of management were clearly visible soon after the system's introduction, and in 1956 it was decided to decentralize and simplify the management and control system. Unfortunately, the first Czechoslovak attempt to reform the economic system in 1958-61 resulted in failure, despite a number of positive elements involved.

The rapid economic development of the 1950s was followed by stagnation during the first half of the 1960s; and in spite of a reduction of investments, this stagnation affected the social and welfare area. This, in turn, led to new reform efforts. A new reform project was published in January 1965: it can be briefly characterized as a 'symbiosis of plan and market'. The first practical reforming steps were taken in 1966 and 1967. During the 'Prague Spring' period, the reform was reviewed and restated as a programme of transition towards a market economy, in which the definition of the role of the plan was qualitatively different from the previous directive system.

The new conception of economic reform was based on the realistic thesis that economic reform can only be successful if it is accompanied by a substantial political reform. The programme of 'revival of socialism', 'socialism with a human face', envisaged, among other changes, the removal of the duplication of management of the economy (by the Communist Party and by the state), full responsibility for the management being allocated to the state authorities.

The programme of reforms was incorporated in the Action Programme of the Communist Party of Czechoslovakia which was issued in April 1968;[10] the role of the state authorities was then defined in the government programme[11] which was based on the Communist Party programme. Both documents accepted the need to change state enterprises into market-driven business entities; they declared a new concept of the role of central economic authorities, defined a rational division of responsibilities between the federal and national republics' authorities in preparation for the change of the state into a federation, suggested the economic tools to be used for securing the fulfilment of the plan, stimulated prognostic work, defined the principles of re-establishing the markets of goods, labour and capital, and prepared the transition to rational pricing, successive demonopolization, and reform of the taxation system.

According to the then prevailing views, small-scale private enterprise was to be permitted, but the private capitalist form of economic management was to remain forbidden. Agricultural co-operative members and workers of state farms showed no interest, in 1968, in returning to private farming. Structural policy was characterized by efforts to scale down the material- and energy-intensive segments of heavy industry (metallurgy, heavy engineering) and to support promising export branches of light and engineering industries and the then neglected areas of the tertiary sector. As to social and welfare functions, the programmes (compared with previous efforts) laid more emphasis on environmental requirements and on reducing working hours.

Before the reform could fully evolve, its further progress was cut short by the armed intervention of five member countries of the Warsaw Pact in August 1968. Though in the early stages of the 'normalization' period it was formally declared that the reform continued, 'free of the revisionist ballast', the regime in fact returned to the previous administrative and directive system of management. Attempts at reform were also stopped in the USSR, Hungary and other countries; consequently, this ruined the programme of economic integration of the CMEA countries of 1971.

The period of 'normalization' saw some partial successes (before 1975) in economic and social policy.[12] Nevertheless, the 'normalizing' regime could not solve the chronic problems that had been aggravated in the 1970s. The gap between Czechoslovakia and the advanced Western countries widened in many areas, including the technical standard and quality of products, modernization of economic structure, competitiveness in world markets, the real purchasing power of the population and in the variation in quality of goods offered on the domestic market. Czechoslovakia was losing its former advantages in some areas of welfare legislation.

According to a sociological survey conducted in mid-1968, the continuing socialist orientation of development was favoured by 89 per cent of the population (the percentage showed a steady growth during the year); 5 per cent of the respondents would have preferred a return to capitalism. Eighty-seven per cent of the people either fully or partly agreed with the policies of the government. Among the ten most popular persons there were eight senior members of the Communist Party (some also holding high posts in the government), and the remaining two were intellectuals who were also members of the Communist Party, though not in the leadership. Beyond any competition, Alexander Dubček, First Secretary of the Central Committee of the Communist Party, ranked first. In 1967, as many as 48 per cent of the population did not believe the Communist Party, but in mid-1968 this proportion had shrunk to 16 per cent, and only 4 per cent of the people asserted an 'absolute lack of trust' in the Party.[13]

The military intervention in Czechoslovakia, followed by 'normalization', met with the general opposition of the populace; however, this opposition sagged during the first half of the 1970s as a result of improving standards of living. However, economic stagnation then replaced growth, and criticism of what was called 'real socialism' intensified: people increasingly opposed the notion that the country was entering a stage of 'advanced socialism'. Frontiers were not closed so tightly as previously, so that Czechoslovaks had more chances to see the differences in economic growth in different countries of the world, and to try to find out how to counter the unfavourable trend. Gorbachev's policy of restructuring was looked at with great expectations by people, though Czechoslovak Communist Party leaders in fact took a reserved or even opposing standpoint, in spite of positive formal declarations.

4. After November 1989

Two attempts to introduce economic reform were made in the 1980s. The first of them, conducted in 1980-81 and officially called 'Improvement of the Management and Planning System', brought no positive results and was later referred to as a reform of the unreformable. The later attempt was called 'Reconstruction of the Economic Mechanism' and was prepared during 1986-88; contemporary sources referred to it as 'the most revolutionary change in the management of economic processes since 1948'. The main measures of the reform were to become effectively early in 1990.[14]

Political changes after November 1989 enabled the state to take an entirely new approach to economic reform. All the significant political forces, including the reformist wing of the Communist Party, were at one in believing that transition to a market-driven economy had to be the main objective of the reform. During the period under the 'National Understanding Government' (until the elections of spring 1990), there was a political consensus in the population's approach to the reform: people were ready to bear sacrifices in making the transition to a market economy a reality. Czechoslovakia was believed to have a better starting position than former CMEA countries, having a higher-performance economy, a higher standard of living, a comparatively high level of education, full self-sufficiency in the production of temperate-zone foodstuffs even at a high level of food consumption, and a low level of foreign debt.

Early in September 1990, the new government published its Economic Reform Scenario.[15] The package of basic economic measures which was to be implemented beginning on 1 January 1991 included the following main elements:

- elimination of subsidies at all levels of production and distribution;
- full liberalization of wholesale and retail prices;
- liberalization of foreign trade, enabling direct foreign trade transactions to all businesses;
- introduction of internal convertibility of the national currency for current account transactions of all domestic economic agents with a market-based exchange rate;
- massive privatization of the majority of enterprises.

Both the Scenario and the later political steps included measures not contained in any of the coalition parties' or movements' programmes (large-scale restitution of property seized by the communist regime in the past, an attempt to solve the issues of ownership of the land, the privatization of forests, a ban on politically motivated nominations to significant posts in the state administration - a measure involving a high number of specialists). The policy of discrimination against agricultural co-operatives (currently the co-operatives represent a decisive proportion of agricultural production) has been a violation of the Scenario's principle of the equality of all forms of ownership within the economy. There have even been voices demanding an expropriation of co-operatives, though there is little interest among co-operative members in returning to private farming.

There is not enough space here to analyse the contents of the Scenario or to enumerate the reform measures. An objective evaluation of economic policy requires some detachment, and also the taking into account of the effect of unpredictable external factors. Though some worsening of the economic situation was predicted, actual developments confirmed the most pessimistic views. The deterioration of the parameters of economic and social development in 1991 was much greater than in any of the years of the economic crisis of the 1930s.[16]

Differentiation of views concerning economic reform was intensifying. Václav Klaus, Minister of Finance, had become a leading personality of the reform. The influential Czech rightist party, the Civic Democratic Party, had been formed around him. The outstanding personalities of the opposition included, for example, Václav Komárek, Deputy Prime Minister in the post-November 'National Consensus Government' and the leading candidate of the Social Democratic Party for the 1992 elections).[17] Social depression, particularly severe in Slovakia, where even the leaders of the ruling right-wing Christian Democratic Party criticised reform; partly under the influence of the Vatican's policy, they emphasized the role of the state in the economy and in social policy, and rejected the extreme manifestations of the capitalist system: these were their arguments against the prevailing Czech liberalism.

Reviewing the developments since November 1989 from the standpoint of the relationship between continuity and discontinuity, it can clearly be seen that discontinuity was needed in many areas, particularly economic mechanisms, the privatization of the property of the state, and the re-orientation of external economic relationships. However, abrupt changes should be avoided where they would endanger the functioning of the economy or where they would unnecessarily affect the social interests of large groups of the population: such developments would undermine the consensus of society and narrow down the social base of the ruling circles. For example, liberalization of prices was introduced on 1 January 1991 in an economic environment dominated by strong monopolies: it failed to bring about the expected effects on enterprises and it has had an adverse effect on the population - directly through a rapid increase in prices and indirectly through the reduction of the value of people's savings. The exchange rate of the Czechoslovak currency, which was considerably undervalued, led to the cheap sale of Czechoslovak property to foreign buyers, to a flow of labour out of the country, and to mass buying of cheap products by foreigners on the Czechoslovak market.[18]

Considerable economic losses have also been caused - as in the 1950s - by placing ideology above economic rationality. Restitutions of property and the efforts to return ownership relations to their position as before 1948 - and in the case of land there are even attempts to return to the status before the establishment of Czechoslovakia in 1918 - destabilize the economy and, in addition, hinder other forms of privatization which are economically sounder. Land often reaches the hands of a second or third generation of heirs of the original owners, often people with no knowledge of or interest in farming. Efforts to break agricultural co-operatives and to re-introduce small-scale private farming could only succeed if they were supported by huge popular pressure. Some experience to this effect was gained in 1991: it suggests that this measure would disrupt all agriculture, thus worsening the conditions of existence for private farmers themselves.

The exaggerated restrictive policy of 1991-92 which has been conducive to a steep decline of production and labour productivity has reduced the resources available for investment and for welfare purposes. This has slowed down the restructuring of the economy, constrained environmental policy and made it necessary to abolish some welfare measures from the past. At the same time, however, the sums of money expended as support to the unemployed show a continuous increase. Owing to the fact that the adverse effects of economic depression have had different intensities in different regions and in different professional groups, conditions have been created for national, social and regional conflicts.

In the situation of 1992, the future development of the Czechoslovak economy was difficult to predict. Optimists and official government forecasts predicted a further worsening in 1992 followed by an improvement later on; however, no one could have said whether the 'social peace' would last so long, and no one dared to predict the results of the elections in spring 1992.[19] At that time it was even unclear whether Czechs and Slovaks would continue living in a common state. By 1 January 1993 they had decided to go their separate ways and the Czech Republic and the Slovak Republic were established.

Notes

1   Butschek, F. (1985), *Die österreichische Wirtschaft im 20. Jahrhundert*, Stuttgart, p. 46.

2   Svennilson, I. (1954), *Growth and Stagnation in the European Economy*, UN, Geneva.

3   Butschek, F., *op. cit.*. pp. 36, 53, (1985), *Historická statistická ročenka ČSSR* , Prague, p. 852.

4   Průcha, V. (ed.), (1982), *Nástin hospodářských dějin v období kapitalismu a socialismu*, (Outline of the economic history of the period of capitalism and socialism), Prague, pp. 140-41, 399.

5   From the point of view of the political orientation of the society, Bulgaria, Yugoslavia and Albania were the closest to the situation in Czechoslovakia in 1945-47. A reverse political spectrum prevailed in Poland, Hungary and Romania.

6   Western historiography sometimes fails clearly to recognize the peculiarities of development in the different countries of Central and Southeastern Europe during the first postwar years. In the case of Czechoslovakia, for example, the effect of the Soviet Army's presence on social changes in the country is sometimes overrated, whereas the internal causes of revolutionary movement are understated.

7   Olšovský, R. & Průcha, V. (eds), (1969), *Stručný hospodářský vývoj Československa do roku 1955*, (Concise economic development of Czechoslovakia until 1955), Prague, pp. 341-3.

8   *Ibid.*, pp. 375, 559.

9   Many leading communist and non-communist economic experts who had expressed their objections against the economic policy were brought into court for forged trials early in the 1950s. The increasing economic difficulties, caused by objective conditions, mistakes in decision making or overestimation of the real possibilities, were all characterized as sabotage. A trial with an 'anti-state conspirator centre', headed by the former General Secretary of the Central Committee of the Communist Party of Czechoslovakia , Rudolf Slánsky, was held in November 1952. It was, for example, stated by the prosecutor, that the defendants had neglected the development of heavy industry, popularized the views concerning a lack of raw materials in Czechoslovakia, developed bottlenecks in production, planned non-efficient investments, maintained the country's dependence on the import of raw materials from capitalist countries, hindered the export to socialist countries by requiring high prices, appointed bourgeois specialists to key posts in the economy, etc. (*Proces s vedením protistátního spikleneckého centra v čele s, Rudolfem Slánským*, [Trials of the leaders of the anti-state conspirator centre headed

by Rudolf Slánský], Prague, 1953, pp. 20-29).

10 (1969), *Rok šedesátý osmý v usneseních a dokumentech ÚV KSČ*, (The year 1968 in resolutions and documents of the Central Committee of the Communist Party of Czechoslovakia), Prague , pp. 103-46.

11 *Rudé Právo*, 25 April 1968.

12 The 1971-75 period was characterized by comparatively high and regular increases in the key economic parameters, by an equilibrium in the balance of trade, by the absence of greater foreign debts, an increasing level of self-sufficiency in food, though food consumption increased, alleviation of an internal lack of economic balance, a good stability of prices, a large volume of new housing (greater than ever before), growth of real wages, and improved social conditions for pensioners and families with young children. The welfare policy contributed to a 'population explosion': late in the 1960s Czechoslovakia was among the countries with the lowest birth rate per 1000 inhabitants, but in 1974-75 Czechoslovakia ranked third in Europe (together with Romania behind Albania and Ireland).

13 *Rudé Právo*, 13 and 18 July 1968.

14 For a description of both attempts, including references to documents, see Průcha, V. (1989), *Ekonomický vývoj Československa a aktuálne otázky hospodárskej politiky*, (Economic development of Czechoslovakia and contemporary questions of economic policy), Bratislava, pp. 181-92, 213-24.

15 Scenario of the Economic and Social Reform. *Hospodářské noviny*, 4 September 1990.

16 According to the Report of the Federal Statistical Bureau, the decrease on an annual average for 1991 compared with the 1990 levels was as follows (per cent): gross domestic product - 15.9; created national income - 19.5; national income utilized - 32.4 (including personal consumption of population - 33.1, accumulation fund - 83.2); investment - 33.8; employment - 11.0; industrial production - 21.2; gross agricultural production - 8.8; construction - 30.5; public goods transport - 23.2; costs of living of household of manual workers and employees + 49.5; nominal money incomes of population in total + 14.5; real money incomes of population - 22.1. Unemployment increased from almost a zero level in 1990 to 6.6 per cent in December 1991. (*Hospodářské noviny*, 7 April 1992, pp. 10-11).

17 In autumn 1991, V. Komárek said in his book *Endangered Revolution* that for the rightist forces now assuming power 'the velvet of the November revolution became unneeded trash ... The rise of these forces if associated with a strengthening orientation of the reform against the people, against the interests of workers and in favour of the new get-rich-quick and future capitalists; this orientation combines with the ideas of social Darwinism of the 19th century and "Law of the Stronger". Hence, this involves increasing activity of the home and foreign speculators,

including the mafias of underhand money changers, receivers of stolen goods, organised gangs involved in economic criminality, claimants to estates - both the original owners and the many heirs, wanting to seize back apartment houses, department stores and shops, industrial companies and even farm land ... the policy pursued by the present Government has become a policy biased towards the interests of a narrow minority élite who wants to develop a wider élite base - in fact an élite business base - to the detriment of the majority of the nation, its standard of living and really democratic equality. This is far beyond the social consensus given by the revolution ... The loss of the consensus, loss of the motive forces of the revolution, means the loss of the chances the revolution offered us. In spite of all the loud declarations on marching towards a market economy, marching to the world, to Europe, such activities are just marking time, going back, exposing this still industrially-strong and well-educated nation to the danger of "balkanization", to the danger of a change into an underdeveloped country where people will have to struggle hard for the basic economic conditions of a decent human life.' Komárek, V. (1991), *Ohrožená revoluce* (*Endangered Revolution*), Bratislava, pp. 35-6.

[18] Comparison of the aggregate costs of living in the Federal Republic of Germany and in Czechoslovakia (including rent, meals in restaurants, public transport fares, medical services etc.) suggests that the DM:Kčs purchase power ratio is 1:3.5-4, though the official exchange rate is 1:16-19. (April 10, 1992).

[19] The parliamentary elections took place at the beginning of June 1992. The turnout was 85 per cent and the final results in the Czech and in the Slovak parts of the state were contradictory. The parties of the government coalition assembled after the elections in 1990 gained in the elections to the national councils (parliaments), 46.5 per cent in the Czech Republic and 26.7 per cent in Slovakia. The data below do not include the parties which were not represented in parliament because they did not reach the required minimum of 5 per cent of the votes cast. This also applies to the two most significant parties of the previous coalition of both Republics, to which the Prime Minister of the Federal Government, M. Čalfa, and the Minister of Foreign Affairs, J. Dienstbier belonged. Thirty-nine parties, coalitions and movements, from which twelve gained more than 5 per cent, stood for parliament. The parties represented in the new federal parliament obtained shares of the vote as follows (the average of the elections to the two Houses of Federal Parliament in the Czech Republic and the Slovak Republic):

	Republic	
A. Rightist and rightist-inclined parties	Czech	Slovak
Civic Democratic Party [a]	33.7	
Christian Democratic Parties	6.0	8.9
Coalition of Hungary Parties		7.4
B. Leftist and leftist-inclined parties		
Left Block Coalition [b]	14.4	
Party of Democratic Left [c]		14.2
Social Democratic Parties [d]	7.2	5.5
Liberal Social Union [e]	6.0	
Movement for Democratic Slovakia [f]		33.7
C. Other parties		
Republican Party [g]	6.4	
Slovak National Party [h]		9.4
D. Parties below the limit of five per cent [i]	26.3	20.9
		16.3
Totals:		
A.	39.7	
B.	27.6	54.3
C.	6.4	9.4
D.	26.3	20.9

(From: (1993), *Statistická ročenka České republiky*, 1993), Prague, pp. 434–40

a) One of the three succession parties of the Civic Forum from 1989, headed by V. Klaus. This party gained very little support in Slovakia. In coalition with it there is the rightist Christian Party, which carries little weight.
b) The Communist Party of Bohemia and Moravia with a few leftist candidates.
c) The Party came into being by transformation from the Communist Party of Slovakia and declared an inclination to a social-democratic orientation.
d) Minimum chances of the Slovak Social Democratic Party were increased when immediately before the election A. Dubček, as its leader, joined it.
e) Coalition of the Agricultural Party, the Czechoslovak Socialist Party and a part of the Green Party.
f) Has a programme to transform Czechoslovakia into a confederation and to correct the implementation of economic reform as outlined by V. Klaus. This reform produced more harmful economic and social consequences for the Slovak Republic in comparison to the Czech Republic. The movement was headed by V. Mečiar, who held the office as Prime Minister of the Slovak Government after the elections in 1990. Under pressure from the

Right he was later recalled from this post; J. Čarnogurský, the Chairman of the rightist Christian Democratic Party, became the Prime Minister of the Slovak Government. This party, strongly Catholic, gained less than 9 per cent of Slovak votes cast.

g) Extreme party, sharply critical of government policy.
h) Separatist party demanding complete separation of Slovakia.
i) The votes of these parties were distributed proportionally, according to results, to those parties that gained more than 5 per cent of votes.

CHAPTER FOUR

Promise, Failure and Prospects of Economic Nationalism in Poland: The Communist Experiment in Retrospect

Henryk Szlajfer

I

In this paper I want to give some thought to how, with the use of analytical categories, it is possible theoretically to understand and interpret Poland's economic experience of 'really existing socialism'. I see three reasons to justify a discussion on this subject.

The first reason, the trivial one, is related to the collapse of the communist planned economy, to the end of an economic, social and political experiment. This end is a signal to historians that a new subject and new sources have appeared and that it is time to set about their homework.

The second reason is not so much related to the 'internal' economic and social history of communist Eastern Europe as to the market economies' own 'internal' history. I do not think that, for instance, the postwar economic history of Western Europe and the rise of the welfare state can be interpreted in isolation from international implications of the existence of communist economies.

The third reason is the most fundamental one as it concerns the way of perceiving the communist economic experiment in its unique historical time and place, it concerns also the definition of this experiment's basic institutions (and their logic). Not without reason and a certain (justified) conceit, historians maintain that it is impossible to understand fully the present conflicts and difficulties in the transition to a market economy without a knowledge of the economic system that is currently receding into the past. Today we see how the lack of this knowledge brings measurable losses, and renders the planning (yes: planning!) of the process of transition, both on the micro- and macro-scale, difficult.

A historical and theoretical interpretation of the communist economic system must not shun stating a definite position of its place in the process of evolution and changes of the European and world economies. I believe that a discussion on the experiment of a planned economy should start from the following hypothesis: communism existed only as a relatively isolated economic system and therefore in a kind of conflict as well as symbiosis with the non-communist world surrounding it.[1] Communism questioned the outside world, but at the same time imitated it and, in the long run, drew on its resources, which allowed the communist system to survive. In a word, despite its declared isolation and distinct features, communism was part and parcel of European and world history. It was a (misdirected) answer to the real problems the market-oriented societies were not able or had no time to solve. In its economic dimension, communism was to a considerable extent both an expression of continuity as well as a negation of the trends and measures preceding its emergence. In my paper I suggest that this overlapping of continuity and negation should be analysed with the use of such categories as *economic nationalism* and *mimetic industrialization.*

II

It would no doubt be fascinating to present the 'episode' of the communist planned economy as a fragment of the Braudelian *'longue durée'* in the perspective of the centuries-long historical process. Questions about the specific nature of this 'episode' would in this perspective be questions about the origins, duration and answers put forward by the specific nature of Eastern and East-Central Europe.[2]

This is not the place to raise a subject as wide as this; nevertheless, one should constantly keep in mind that the phenomenon which lay at the foundation of the communist experiment - the division of the European economy into developed and backward areas - by no means appeared as late as in the twentieth or nineteenth century. The processes of consolidation of modern capitalist development at the turn of the nineteenth century only widened the already existing basic differences between Eastern and Western Europe.

To bring back that period is of great significance in a discussion of the planned economy, understood as both economic nationalism as well as mimetic industrialization. It was in that period that the old 'British model' of industrialization was transformed into 'Bismarckian' development. The functional and institutional separation of the capital goods sector (in the vocabulary of 'really existing socialism', heavy industry) is this model's characteristic trait.[3] This fact changes fundamentally the *initial conditions* of industrial development and the methods of its diffusion, the distribution of related costs (making industrial development more expensive) and the role of the state.[4] Examples which symbolize this transformation are very well known: Germany, to some extent Japan, and needless to say tsarist Russia in the 'Witte period'.

The area of central Poland which constituted a part of the tsarist empire at the time was affected by these fundamental changes only to a limited extent. The Kingdom of Poland went in for 'industrialization from above' earlier and with no success.[5] As a result at the turn of the nineteenth century, up until the First World War, the economy of central Poland remained a peculiar 'intermediary zone between industrial and agricultural Europe',[6] an area of intensive import-substitution industrialization with regard to non-durable consumer goods, and an importer of both capital and intermediary goods. What made her different from, for example, Latin American countries at that time and later, was not merely her much more highly developed import-substitution industrialization, but the absence of a strong and influential alliance of social forces promoting export specialization, which would include miners, merchants, landowners and industrialists involved in servicing the export economy.[7]

Poland gained her independence in 1918, as a peculiar economic hybrid. The country's economic space comprised areas which were not integrated with one another, and which were taken over from Russia, Austria-Hungary and Germany: enclaves of modern heavy industry in Upper Silesia and large areas of backward farming and handicraft in central and eastern parts of the country. At the same time, Poland did not exemplify a typical export economy - despite the strong political and economic influence of agrarian interests: what is more, she had at her disposal relatively large raw material resources and consumer goods industries, as well as educated elites, in the state apparatus and in the army in particular. The hybrid nature of the Polish economy and society somehow made it difficult to see the problem of backwardness sharply, and in the political sphere, it helped Poles to cherish a number of 'big power' illusions.

On the other hand, the need for economic integration after 1918 and the costs and difficulties involved, followed by the shock of the Great Depression, set in motion in Poland mechanisms that fed the ideology and policy of economic nationalism. 'Agents' of such policy - state bureaucracy and the army - appeared. The needs of the day were both the demolition of the hybrid economic structure (e.g. projects to narrow inter-regional economic differences) and the building up of the missing link in the economic structure - strong capital goods industries, first and foremost steel, engineering, mechanical, transport, electrical and chemical industries.

The construction of the Central Industrial Region (COP) in the second half of the 1930s, in the backward but strategically important area of southeastern Poland, was the most impressive example of economic nationalism. At the same time, the idea of economic planning stopped being an exotic 'novelty', particularly to circles under the direct influence of Vice Premier Eugeniusz Kwiatkowski who was clearly fascinated by the Soviet experiment in central planning.[8]

The policy of economic nationalism, which included elements of macroeconomic planning, enabled the Polish elites to attempt to resolve the dilemmas related to the construction of an integrated economic space with a wide range of industries. 'For ages and ages', wrote Kwiatkowski, 'we have been a nation of farmers: today we must become a multipurpose nation, a society of businessmen, farmers, blue- and white-collar workers'.[9] *Nationalism, the state, planning, heavy industry*, these basic elements of the new economic *Weltanschauung* were an answer both to the challenge of backwardness and the 'Bismarckian' model of industrialization and the disintegration of the world economy.

The attitude, hostile at the time, of foreign capital towards plans to establish 'artificial' industries in Poland also mattered in the creation of a new economic ideology, and affected the pace of industrialization. Foreign capital's modest share in the process of the country's industrialization in the 1930s posed the problem of *internal* sources of finance for new industries.[10]

However, at the initial stage of development of new industries, the problem was not yet acute enough to require drastic decisions. Nevertheless, Poles began to stress the need to rely more on the country's own resources and to defend its economic sovereignty, although major decision makers rejected extreme notions of total self-sufficiency. Both Manoilescu in Romania and the less theoretically-oriented Kwiatkowski in Poland interpreted economic nationalism, and demands for industrialization and for a more balanced domestic economy, as a (future) extension of their respective countries' participation in the international economy.

III

The economic nationalism which appeared in the period discussed, and which was to play a special role after the Second World War, was a *holistic nationalism*. Unlike *particular nationalism*, it referred not to the interests of particular industries, but to the economy as a whole. Holistic nationalism was a kind of modernized Listian vision of 'harmony of productive powers', a harmony of agriculture and industry, adjusted to new circumstances.[11]

In the economic literature of the time this kind of nationalism was well described by Wilhelm Roepke, who observed, 'Under the influence of the ideal of national economic stabilization, dominating all other goals of economic policy, economic nationalism has ceased to be limited in aim and character, and now it tends to become "total" [...] with a view to supporting or to making possible a policy of regulating the national economic process as a whole'.[12] Put in a nutshell, the differences between the two nationalisms were as follows: in the case of particular nationalism we deal with vested interests (industries, sectors or even large individual firms) tending to colonize the state and the economy; in the case of holistic nationalism we observe a different tendency - the state bureaucracy 'etatize nationalism',[13]and try to colonize private interests in the name of building a sovereign and fully-developed national economy.

However, unlike the holistic nationalism in Germany or Japan, holistic nationalism in Poland appeared not so much as an instrument of a big power's territorial expansion as a result of the country's economic backwardness. The Great Depression was a turning point in this regard. It very painfully showed the economic vulnerability and non-sovereignty of the economic structure that existed in Poland, and the uselessness of liberal economic theories when it came to coping with urgent economic problems. At the same time, the country's internal weakness was perceived and analysed in a wider, international context: Kwiatkowski, among others, demonstrated that 'crises affecting raw and intermediate materials are much more severe and longer than those affecting the finished product [...] Therefore it is here [...] where the basic problem of the internal restructuring of the Polish economy lies'.[14]

In prewar Poland, holistic economic nationalism did not acquire a fully shaped form, either in practice or as a doctrine. It was a promise whose fulfilment was frustrated by the outbreak of the Second World War. Therefore it is impossible to assess its practical effects. All the same, one can propound a thesis that this kind of nationalism did not play an entirely negative role, and that perhaps it offered certain good long-term development prospects.[15] What is more, it was a short-term solution for the backward countries which the world crisis affected particularly strongly. The statistical data available show that those backward countries which in the 1930s opted for a radical variant of economic nationalism performed better.[16] This applies both to East-Central Europe and to Latin America.

Polish economic nationalism was of a rather mild variety, especially during the first, most dramatic, stage of the Great Depression. To a certain degree, this fact decided the depth and the duration of the internal crisis.[17] Both communists and 'technocrats' from the old state apparatus remembered that experience well (after 1945 some of the latter found employment with the Central Planning Office (CUP) and with the Ministry of Industry and Trade).

The holistic nationalism of the interwar period was not merely a promise. The 'economic philosophy' of this nationalism, monstrously exaggerated, emerged as one of the building blocks of the communist planned economy. I mean here first and foremost the tendency to subordinate private interests to the emerging 'state technostructure'[18] which was progressively developing towards a particular etatist synthesis. However, in the interwar period, the transformation from the interventionist *regulation-making state* to the fully fledged *production-making and controlling state* did not take place. The holistic nationalism of that period stopped despite all the authoritarian and/or totalitarian temptations at the border of private property (at least of those of its own citizens who were not 'alien').[19] Another important element of the interwar legacy of holistic nationalism was a tendency to combine the policies of economic nationalism with the imposition of corporatist social, economic and political institutions - the latter being treated both as prerequisites for national integration and as an instrument to increase the effectiveness of national economic policy.

IV

The Second World War on the one hand compromised the fascist variant of the command economy; on the other, however, it somehow legitimized the command economy's communist variant. The presence of Soviet tanks in Berlin alone seemed a sufficient indication of the enormous economic viability of the communist experiment. Planning became fashionable, all the more so because in the eyes of liberal democracies it was justified by Keynes's employment theory, which implied a certain degree of socialization of investments.[20] In the light of the interwar experience of state interventionism and war-economy planning, statism was no longer a threat. Quite the reverse; etatism, added to war devastation and inherited backwardness, fertilized the ground for the acceptance of new collectivism, defined and propagated as a shortcut in the struggle against backwardness. The ideas of regulating international trade, of subordinating it to the requirements of internal develolpment, did not encounter much resistance. In this respect, particular emphasis was given to the bitter experience of the inter-war period, and the idea of organizing a self-sufficient, semi-closed economy seemed especially attractive.

It goes without saying that the tendencies described above acquired a different character in market economies than in Poland controlled by a communist elite backed by Soviet tanks. All the same, here and there the climate was congenial. It is worth noting that the draft long-term economic plan prepared in 1947 by the Polish Central Planning Office, which was controlled not by communists but by socialists, included the following provision: 'The entire economy shall be oriented towards supplying the home market and towards increasing the per capita income consumed. The volume of exports shall depend on import requirements.'[21] For all practical purposes, we find in this draft plan all the basic elements of the ideal of economic nationalism: match resources with internal demand, subordinate foreign trade to domestic needs and to the demand profile, trade in surpluses, immunize the economy against the influence of the world market, and start planning.

However, one element was missing, one which determined the future of both the CUP and the idea of a consumer-oriented economic plan. What was missing was a distinct pressure on intensive industrialization, on the building of heavy industry, including the defence industry. A firm stress on the need for macro-economic planning in the Soviet fashion was also missing. Of course, Polish socialists did not repudiate either the need for industrialization or for urgent macro-economic planning. However, what mattered was where the emphasis was laid. The option taken up by communists was pellucid: copy the Soviet model, go for a radical variant of etatism without any dubious experiments with the 'mixed economy' which can only make total control over the economy more difficult, start building heavy industry. If we look at the problem in a comparative perspective, we cannot fail to notice that the presence of Soviet tanks in Berlin was a convincing economic argument, even for those who had broken with Stalin. The example of Yugoslavia, which before and for several years after the breach with the Soviet Union, developed in keeping with the 'general' Eastern European pattern,[22] shows that the Soviet model had some attractions, not limited to external pressure or ideological imitation alone.

The primary attraction was a vision of economic sovereignty, understood in radically autarchic categories as an answer to both many centuries of underdevelopment and to capitalism ('the West').[23] That vision was particularly attractive to the communist elite in Poland, the country which, in view of her size, natural resources, population and ownership of industrialized Upper Silesia, seemed to be ideally prepared to copy the Soviet model of industrialization and to make the autarchic Utopia come true. Zbigniew M. Fallenbuchl is right to observe that the economic nationalism of Polish communists in the past four decades expressed itself in 'a relatively high degree of rigidity in respect of development strategy and the basic economic system' and that meant 'a continuous insistence on economic self-sufficiency and for constructing heavy industry'.[24] I think it was no accident that the other East-Central European country to try to copy the Soviet model almost exactly was Romania, the country with a resources endowment similar to that of Poland. In 1988, these two countries were the Soviet bloc's economically most closed (save the Soviet Union itself), if one measures the degree of closeness by the proportion of exports in the GNP.[25] The then attractiveness of the Soviet model is also testified to by the fact that as late as the mid-1980s in an academic publication one could read: 'Industrialization of Poland and of other people's democracies, was right to imitate the strategy worked out during the industrialization of the USSR.'[26] Although in the next sentence the author makes a reservation that this 'correct' strategy was combined in practice with 'negative tendencies towards [achieving] the highest possible degree of self-sufficiency',[27] this only shows that the author does not grasp the logic of Soviet industrialization at all.

V

The Polish model of a communist economy differed in many respects from the Soviet one. To mention one such difference should suffice. In contrast to the Soviet Union, industrialization in Poland did not take place on the debris of private farming. According to Stalinist standards, the collectivization started in Poland at the beginning of the 1950s and was carried out in an extremely sluggish manner. As a result, there was a fiscal squeeze on peasants, but not a wholesale assault on private land ownership. In 1953, the peak year of the Polish industrial drive and of Polish Stalinism, more than 80.4 per cent of farmland remained in private hands.[28] Therefore one can justify a hypothesis that, contrary to the Soviet 'primitive accumulation', Polish industrialization was based on urban resources to a much greater extent.

Yet, this difference did not defy the bare logic of the communist variant of holistic economic nationalism which was copied from the Soviet Union. That logic applied both to the institutional framework as well as to the basic strategic lines of development. What really made the Polish model of economic nationalism different was the way in which the Polish communist elites tried to cope with the problem of modernization once the developmental dynamics started during the six-year plan were exhausted. To put it briefly: the Polish model amazingly combined the 'orthodox' fascination with self-sufficiency with a degree of political openness and, in the 1970s, with an attempt to open the country rapidly to the world economy and to accomplish another 'technological acceleration'. Also, in Poland the mimetic character of industrialization was more distinct - the gap between the internal mechanisms to induce and control accumulation and the external sources of innovation.

VI

The key characteristics of Soviet holistic nationalism and its Polish variant can be presented in the following points:

1. The destruction of the institutional framework of private property. In the language of the theory of 'property rights' this can be expressed as the

total elimination of the difference between private benefits and the costs of government protection on the one hand, and social and private benefits on the other, and hence the complete disappearance of the category of economic costs.[29] To compensate for this 'loss', an attempt was made to implement the widespread use, among other notions, of so-called 'technologically justified norms' and other forms of calculus in physical units.[30] It was a peculiarly Polish attribute that both in the countryside and in the town private sectors existed, although in the case of the latter, Poland's 'comparative advantage' was not all that apparent (especially in comparison with East Germany). However, this 'peculiarity' can hardly be recognized as an introduction to economic rationality or as the basic *economic* specificity of the *modus operandi* of the Polish variant of holistic nationalism. The private sector suffered a gradual degeneration, particularly in towns, without exerting any major impact on strategic decisions. One cannot therefore be surprised by the opinion expressed by the Polish representative of Curtis International, who argues that the sector 'had nothing or nearly nothing to do with market economy'.[31]

2. The absence of the institution of private property led to the omnipotence of the state and to the increase of the potential magnitude of errors in micro- and macro-economic decisions. As concerned strategic choices that meant, among other things, moulding development by the more or less intuitive copying of Western development patterns in the Polish case, often known only second-hand through the mediation of the USSR, particularly in the 1950s. This unfocused approach found its concrete expression in ineffectiveness of macro-economic planning. Comparative analysis of the four long-term plans from the years 1950 to 1970 shows that under none of them was the planned growth in agricultural production achieved, that under each of them the planned level of industrial production was surpassed and that under three of them the planned level of real wages and of national income was not attained.[32] Analysis of the period between 1947 and 1980 produces a similar picture, with the most serious deviations from the respective plan being recorded in the years 1950-55 and 1971-80,[33] i.e. in the two periods of the most rapid, though based on different resources, developmental acceleration. Today, certain Polish economists, having in mind the 1970s and 1980s in particular, maintain with reason that 'in point of fact, there was neither plan nor market' at the time, but only a highly-centralized command economy.[34]

3. Heavy industry (in which defence industries had a considerable share) was the centre of gravity of the first stage of Polish industrialization, in the years 1950-55. Concentration on heavy industry led to a number of structural disequilibria, especially with regard to raw materials. As a result, at the second stage of industrialization, which started in 1958-60, in conformity with the ideal of self-sufficiency, development of the raw materials base became a basic priority, which meant a further consolidation of the primacy of the so-called 'A' group (heavy industry). The discussion Michal Kalecki started at the end of the 1950s on the

perspective plan for the years 1961-75 did not lead, despite his efforts, to any real alternative: in particular, 'no concept of Poland's specialization with a view to the world market' was put forward.[35] The primacy of development of the raw material industries and of achieving self-sufficiency in, among other things, cereal production involved highly capital-intensive investments which only consolidated the development model adopted in the 1950s. As a result, 'changes in the structure of industrial investments in the years 1950-58 and in 1959-1967, only to a very small degree made our structure resemble that of highly industrialized countries, and in some respects, made it even more dissimilar from the one prevailing in the West'.[36] The Polish economy entered a vicious circle: 'the overgrowth of manufacturing industries forced the overgrowth of extractive industries'.[37] It seems that it was exactly at the second stage of industrialization that the institutional shape of communist economic nationalism began to exert a direct negative impact on the evolution of the industrial macro-structure. The mimetic industrialization of the mid-1950s, irrespective of the destruction of the institutional bases of a rational economic choice, in principle allowed for the copying of the traditional - 'Bismarckian' - structure of Western European industry. Then, intersectoral transfers of resources and their allocation to manufacturing allowed for a relatively high increase in labour productivity, in national income and in industrial output, and for reducing the Polish divergence from some Western European countries.[38] In the years 1951-55, labour productivity rose by an average of 7 per cent a year: in the following fifteen years, it plummeted steadily. It was only in the 1970s that the rise in labour productivity accelerated again,[39] this time, however, as a direct result of an economic opening to the outside world and the credit bonanza.

4. During the rapid industrialization drive, substantial imports of technology and equipment were absolutely necessary. For some of the industries established in the USSR in the first half of the 1930s, such imports provided for nearly 100 per cent of their equipment.[40] In the case of Poland in the first half of the 1950s, imports made up almost 60 per cent of the total investment in machinery and equipment.[41] Therefore I cannot agree with the statement that the Stalinist model of industrialization assumed an anti-import policy at every stage.[42] On the contrary, without imports at the initial stage of acceleration, Stalinist industrialization would be out of the question entirely. When for primarily ideological and political reasons the communist elites opposed capital co-operation (joint ventures etc.), they still favoured technical cooperation financed by trade,[43] treating the latter as a strategic element of their industrialization policy. This is why we can describe the Soviet model as copied by Poland as a particular variant of import-led growth.[44] Such a growth is fully compatible with the ideal of economic nationalism as presented in the classic work by List. It does not contradict the logic of import-substitution industrialization either. The differences between the two occur elsewhere. They are related to the above-mentioned first key feature of the planned

economy, its new institutional framework and its long-term developmental consequences.

5. At the stabilization stage which followed the rapid acceleration of the first half of the 1930s, the Soviet Union drastically curtailed its foreign trade and switched over to a closed system. The previously obtained injection of technical progress made it possible to 'consume' the benefits from the investment drive without maintaining any close contacts with the outside world. In the case of Poland, the slide towards autarchy was much less violent owing to Poland's want of many raw materials and manufactures, and also to the new international situation. These differences were, however, those of degree not of quality: they did not bring about any fundamental change to the adopted strategy of development of industry and the economy as a whole. The belief in the necessity of growth on every 'front' prevailed despite the fainthearted attempts in the 1960s at arriving at a concept of export specialization. In that period too, an idea arose of establishing a peculiar 'export enclave' based on 100 firms successful in exporting to the West;[45] at the same time the average annual rate of growth in exports to the West in the years 1961-70 was driven up to 9.3 per cent.[46] On the other hand, the avoidance of foreign debt remained a dogma, and imports of Western technologies were continuously treated with suspicion.[47]

At the time when the Polish economy was passing to the stabilization stage and then to the rapid development of raw materials industries (1958-70), it missed the historical opportunity to join the brisk expansion of the world economy and trade which lasted until the beginning of the 1970s. The attempt to catch up, started in the 1970s, ended in total failure, despite the considerable infusion of new technologies. The average rate of growth of exports to the West in that decade was 6.7 per cent, i.e less than in the 1960s.[48] Even if we take a cautious attitude towards any prognoses, it is useful to refer here to estimates giving us an idea of the width of the Polish economy's 1988 'export gap', due to the anachronistic semi-closed system. According to those estimates, assuming the current income level, the opening of the system based on nationalistic principles would have required a rise in export value from $14 billion to more than $39 billion, as well as a radical change in the geographical directions of foreign trade.[49]

This 'gap' to a certain extent symbolizes the legacy the Polish economy must handle today. The 1970s were the time of an attempt at a conservative modernization of the semi-closed economy by means of an uncontrolled entry into the international structure of trade and finance. The *style* of that entry looked exactly like the Latin American 'dance of millions' in the 1920s. Perhaps such a style was inevitable in view of the economic and political elites' inexperience in international economic relations.[50] All the more so in that the opening of the Polish economy took place via the influx of banking, not industrial capital, hence allowing the Polish elites relative freedom in the allocation of external financial resources (with resultant waste of these funds), the consolidation of traditional exports, limitations on the effect of the opening on the improvement of the technological standard of industry and on the setting in motion of a mechanism to ensure a steady flow of future innovations. The transformation potential of the 'opening', if measured by the rise in the competitiveness of the Polish economy or by the development of modern export industries, was not great. As a result, the first open 'clash' between the semi-closed economy and the world market ended in the total defeat of the former.

That 'clash' was a lesson Poland did not understand, which became obvious only in January 1990 when the so-called shock therapy was undertaken. I mean here primarily the *costs involved in the transformation* of the semi-closed into the market economy. The defeat suffered in the 1970s meant the failure to transform the inherited system, a failure of both the elites and society. At the foundation of this defeat is a very clear economic and social syndrome, established in previous decades. This can be briefly described as a coincidence of lunatic relative costs and prices, of the system of consumer investment and developmental preferences, and of the social safety net typical of the semi-closed economy. The syndrome's economic aspect is exposed by the study of the 1988 ratio of value added at world prices to the domestic output price in the industries of Poland, Hungary and Czechoslovakia. The study reveals both a weak correlation between the domestic value added and the value added at world prices, as well as a negative value added at world prices in about 24 per cent of Polish manufacturing industry's potential. In the case of Poland, the single most important factor contributing to this state of affairs was the extremely uneconomic price of energy.[51] To do away with this syndrome required a veritable revolution and such a revolution was started in Poland in 1990.

The revolution's final outcome cannot be predicted as yet, and therefore it would be premature to announce the death of economic nationalism.[52] Behind the economic aspect of the nationalist syndrome are definite interests. Their social dimension was depicted accurately by Valtr Komárek, until June 1990 the chief of the Czechoslovak government's economic team: 'The revolution was not undertaken so people would live worse than under communism.'[53] In Poland not only the majority of the public but also that group of economists who prepared the 'shock therapy' strategy were under the illusion that the nationalist economic syndrome could be broken up relatively quickly. In January 1990, when the 'therapy' was started, people believed that success was a matter of several months, not years.

In reality, however, the economic deprivation of a considerable part of the population seems to be one of those costs of transformation that cannot be avoided. The time this systemic transformation will take will not be short. These two factors are conducive to the crystallization and consolidation of group interests centred on those sectors and industries which are particularly endangered by the policy of economic liberalization and opening up to foreign competition. These endangered groups include a considerable number of peasants and employees of heavy industry (together with the defence industry). The *lingua franca* of the social groups and the elites connected with these endangered sectors is the language and slogans of economic and political nationalism. The holistic economic nationalism of the communist period is still alive and kicking, because the whole economic structure inherited from communism is still with us and breeding nationalistic reactions.

'Shock therapy' and the conviction that economic nationalism is not a rational answer to the problems of systemic transformation are not enough. To extricate ourselves from communist holistic nationalism requires more than that. It requires the establishment of a clear link between transformation and the provision of basic needs and an efficient social safety net:[54] it also requires the elaboration of new links between state intervention and the (emerging market) economy. If reformers do not establish such links, popular support for demagogic economic nationalists is to be expected soon. The acceptance of their demagogy will for some people be a matter of life, not merely choice.[55]

Notes

1   Von Laue, T. H. (ed.), (1987), *The World Revolution of Westernization. The Twentieth Century in Global Perspective*, New York.

2   See the historiosophical reflections by Bibo, I. (1991), *Democracy, Revolution, Self-Determination. Selected Writings*, New York.

3   For an attempt at a theoretical and empirical interpretation of this crucial transformation, see the famous typology by Hoffman, W.G. (1958), *The Growth of Industrial Economies*. Manchester (1st German ed. 1931).

4   See Rosenberg, N. (1976), *Perspectives on Technology*, London.

5   See Jedlicki, J. (1964), *Nieudana proba kapitalistycznej industrializacji. Analiza panstwowego gospodarstwa przemyslowego w Krolestwie Polskim XIX w*, Warsaw.

6   Ihnatowicz, I. (1982), 'Przemysl handel finanse' in Kieniewicz, S. (ed.), *Polska XIX wieku. Panstwo, spoleczenstwo, kultura*, Warsaw, p. 88.

7   For more on this subject, see Szlajfer, H. (1991), 'Enforced Industrialization: The Contrasting Examples of the Kingdom of Poland and Latin America in the First Half of the Nineteenth Century', in Batou, J. (ed.), *Between Development and Underdevelopment. The Precocious Attempts at Industrialization of the Periphery 1800-1870*, Geneva.

8   Kwiatkowski, E. (1989), *Dysproporcje. Rzecz o Polsce przeszlej i obecnej*. Warsaw. (1st ed. 1931), p. 242f.

9   *Ibid.*

10 Foreign capital's share in the financing of the investment plan in the years 1936-39 was below 6.7 per cent. Drozdowski, M.M. (1963), *Polityka gospodarcza rzadu polskiego 1936-1939*, Warsaw, p. 136f.

11 List, F. (1922), *The National System of Political Economy*. London. See also Szlajfer, H. (1990), 'Economic Nationalism of the Peripheries as a Research Problem', in *idem* (ed.), *Economic Nationalism in East-Central Europe and South America 1918-1939*, Geneva.

12 Roepke, W. (1941), *International Economic Disintegration.*, London, p. 202.

13 Sugar, P.F. (1988), 'Zrodla i tradicje nacjonalizmu w Europie Wschodniej'. *Aneks*. No. 50, p. 133, is right when he emphasizes that in the interwar period, nationalism in East-Central Europe was both 'centred on the state' as well as 'officially determined'. Yet he does not relate this tendency specifically to the policy of holistic economic nationalism, which I find quite surprising.

14 Kwiatkowski, E. *op. cit.*, p. 292.

15 See the pathbreaking study by Kofman, J. (1992), *Nacjonalizm gospodarczy - szansa czy bariera rozwoju. Przypadek Europy Srodkowo-*

Wschodniej w okresie miedzywojennym., Warsaw.

[16] For one of the most recent contributions to the subject, see Eichengreen, B. & Portes, R. (1990), 'The Interwar Debt Crisis and its Aftermath'. *The World Bank Research* Observer, 5, 1.

[17] See Kofman, J. *op. cit.*

[18] Ianni, Q. (1971), *Estado e planejamento economico no Brasil 1930-1970.*, Rio de Janeiro, pp. 4-5.

[19] Turner, H.A. Jr, (1985), writes: 'Germany's businessmen experienced little difficulty in adapting to a [Nazi] regime that, even though it gave them no voice in its decision, held labor in check and, on the whole, respected private property'. *German Big Business and the Rise of Hitler*, New York, p. 338. For Italy, see Gregor, A.J. (1979), *Italian Fascism and Developmental Dictatorship*, Princeton, NJ.

[20] During the war, the Polish London-based government-in-exile carried on intensive work on a long-term plan for economic development, which Kwiatkowski started already before the war. See (1989), *Problemy gospodarcze Drugiej Rzeczypospolitej*, Warsaw, pp. 342-52.

[21] CUP, 'Wytyczne planu dlugoterminowego na lata 1950-1973' in Jedruszczak, H. (ed.), (1983), *Wizje gospodarki socjalistycznej w Polsce 1945-1949. Materialy zrodlowe.* Warsaw, p. 438.

[22] See Dyker, D.A. (1990), *Yugoslavia: Socialism, Development and Debt*, London and New York.

[23] In the early 1950s, the Polish communist leader Boleslaw Bierut stated this two-fold goal clearly in a number of his speeches. See Karpiński, A. (1986), *40 lat planowania w Polsce. Problemy, ludzie, refleksje*, Warsaw, p. 49. For Hungary, see Berend, I.T. (1990), *The Hungarian Economic Reforms 1953-1988* , Cambridge, p. 7. To explain the origins of the communist autarchy by referring to the role the communist elites attributed, for example, to defence determinants is not, of course, wrong. According to some estimates, the share of military expenditures in Poland's national income in the years 1950-54 was around 15 per cent; at the same time in Hungary, investments in the defence industry were calculated at 33-50 per cent of the total investment fund. See Muller, A. (1985), 'Przyspieszony wzrost gospodarczy w latach 1971-75 a proporcje wzrostu w trzydziestoleciu 1950-1980', in *idem* (ed.), *U zrodel polskiego kryzysu. Spoleczno-ekonomiczne uwarunkowania rozwoju gospodarczego Polski w latach osiemdziesiatych*, Warsaw, p. 102 and Berend, I.T. *op. cit.* On the other hand, however, this factor hardly explains the continuity of the basic structures of the growth strategies and of macro-economic proportions established at the early stage of the communist industrialization. This is why I maintain that the expansion of the military sector, especially in small and medium-size communist countries, only dramatized the basic problem of how to handle the

'questions' of backwardness and of capitalism.

[24] Fallenbuchl, Z.M. (1989), 'Economic Nationalism in the Eastern Block Countries', *Canadian Review of Studies in Nationalism*, Vol. XVI, 1-2, p. 160.

[25] Collins, S.M. & Rodrik, D. (1991), *Eastern Europe and the Soviet Union in the World Economy*, Washington, DC, p. 9.

[26] Wilczewski, R. 'Rozwoj przemyslu w Polsce w latach 1947-1955', in Kaliński, J. & Landau, Z. (eds.), (1986), *Gospodarka Polski Ludowej 1944-1955*, Warsaw, p. 224. (2nd ed.).

[27] *Ibid.*

[28] Kostrowicka, I. 'Rozwoj rolnictwa w latach 1947-1955' in Kaliński & Landau, *op. cit.*, p. 272. The six-year plan approved by the Sejm in 1950 ('after consultations' with the Soviet authorities), provided that collectivization would extend not to 22 but to 40 per cent of the farmland. Karpiński, Z. *op. cit.* p. 55f.

[29] See North, D.C. & Thomas, R.P. (1973), *The Rise of the Western World. A New Economic History*, Cambridge. Compare the considerations on the 'logic of a closed system' presented by Kaminski, B. (1991), *The Collapse of State Socialism: The Case of Poland*, Princeton, NJ.

[30] The appearance of computer techniques strengthened the illusion that it was possible to arrive at correct relative prices while by-passing the market completely. Oskar Lange was one of those outstanding Polish economists who cherished such an illusion.

[31] (1992), *Wprost*, March 1, p. 12.

[32] Jezierski, A., 'Przemiany gospodarcze w PRL' in Topolski, J. (ed.), (1987), *Kierunki rozwoju Polski po drugiej wojnie swiatowej*, Poznan, p. 69.

[33] Karpiński, *op. cit.* pp. 391-7.

[34] Wilczynski, W. *et. al..* (1992), *Drogi wyjscia z polskiego kryzysu gospodarczego.*, Warsaw-Poznan, p. 14.

[35] Karpiński, *op. cit.* p.115. See also Osiatynski, J. (1988), *Michal Kalecki o gospodarce socjalistycznej*, Warsaw.

[36] Karpiński, A. (1969), *Polityka uprzemyslowienia Polski w latach 1958-1968*, Warsaw, p. 87. In the years 1950-75, the share of the 'A' group in the total industrial product rose from 53.1 per cent to 68.0 per cent. See Muller, *op. cit.*, p. 169.

[37] Winiecki, J. (1988), *The Distorted World of Soviet-Type Economies*, London and New York, p. 90. See also Muller, *op. cit.*

[38] For example, Eva Ehrlich reckons that compared to Italy and Spain, Poland's position had been improving until 1960, and rapidly declined after that year. Quoted after Marer, P. 'The Economies and Trade of

Eastern Europe' in Griffith, W.E. (ed.) (1989), *Central and Eastern Europe: The Opening Curtain?*, Boulder, CO, p. 49.

39 Muller, *op. cit.*, p. 127.

40 See Sutton, A.C. (1971), *Western Technology in Soviet Economic Development 1930-1945*, Stanford, CA

41 Wojciechowski, B. 'Handel zagraniczny Polski' in Kaliński and Landau, *op. cit.*, p. 383.

42 See for example, Landau, Z. 'Glowne tendencje rozwoju gospodarczego Polski Ludowej' in Muller, A. (ed.) *op. cit.*, p. 53f. For an opposite view see Winiecki, *op. cit.* and the ample literature on the import-substitution strategies of industrialization in underdeveloped countries.

43 See Woroniecki, J. (1990), *Obcy kapital w gospodarce radzieckiej. Doswiadczenia i wspolczesnosc*, Warsaw, p. 150.

44 See Gomulka, S. 'Growth and the Import of Technology: Poland 1971-1980', *Cambridge Journal of Economics* 2(1978), 1. With certain modifications, Gomulka's interpretation of the 1970s can be applied to the analysis of the investment drive in the first half of the 1950s.

45 Karpiński, *op. cit.* p. 154f.

46 Rydygier, W. 'Pulapka zadluzenia' in Muller, (ed.) *op. cit.*, p. 279.

47 In the years 1945-70, Poland acquired a mere 217 licences (primarily for heavy industry) against 428 licences purchased in the next decade. On the other hand, at the end of 1970, her foreign debt stood at about $1 billion, whereas the sums accumulated in the so-called Reserve Foreign Currency fund were above $0.6 billion. Karpiński, *op. cit.* p. 170.

48 Rydygier, *op. cit.*, p. 279.

49 Collins and Rodrik, *op. cit.*, pp. 34 and 40.

50 This suppostion is partly confirmed by the evidence included in (1986), *Protokoly tzw komisji Grabskiego*, Paryz, which is a record of the 'Party investigation' against Gierek and his closest associates carried out in 1981.

51 Hughes, G. & Hare, P. (1991), 'Competitiveness and Industrial Restructuring in Czechoslovakia, Hungary and Poland'. *European Economy*, No. 2 (special edition).

52 With different intensity and in a framework of radically opposite 'ideological discourses' economic nationalism is advocated in post-communist Poland by both the extreme Left and the extreme Right. See, for example, Dymkowski, R. (1992), 'Nacjonalizm gospodarczy i samorzadnosc pracownicza'. *Tygodnik Antyrzadowy*, No. 14 (April)

53 (1992), *Newsweek*, March 9.

54 This is clearly the message included in John Williamson's elaboration on the 'Washington Consensus' concerning a 'sound policy' of economic transition. See his presentation to the conference on 'Economic

Liberalization and Democratic Consolidation' organized by the Social Science Research Council and CEDES. Forli, 2-4, April 1992.

55 I propounded this conclusion several years ago in May 1990, to a conference organized at Pultusk (Poland) by the East European Research Group. I do not modify this conclusion now because what seemed to be croaking then is today a mere fact of life.

CHAPTER FIVE

The Rise and Fall of Yugoslavia: An Economic History View

Franjo Štiblar

1. Introduction

The rise and fall of Yugoslavia can be to a great extent attributed to economic factors, although political, ethnic, national, social, demographic and other determinants played a major role. It is unfortunate that economic factors have not been recognized as relevant to the destiny of the country. For large-scale communism (socialism), the inability of the system to deliver sustained long-term economic development caused its defeat in competition with capitalist systems.

I do not dismiss significant national, religious, ethnic, cultural, social and other differences between Yugoslav federal units as causes of the country's disintegration. With economic success the conflict could probably have been kept under control longer, but not forever; these differences survived more than half a century of homogenization efforts. Apparently, some of the basic premises in the creation of Yugoslavia were wrong. As external dangers disappeared with warming East-West relations and internal economic failures undermined the material basis for symbiosis between the workers and the Communist Party elite, workers' support for the regime as a *quid pro quo* for social security provided by the leadership diminished the centrifugal forces due to the above-mentioned differences surfaced again and the collapse of the Yugoslav Federation (in its existing form) inevitably followed.

The Yugoslav regime managed to remain stable because of *de facto* exclusion of large segments of society from public involvement and decision making: intellectuals were disqualified as extremists, managers as power seekers, religious activists as reactionaries and nationally aware people as separatists, irredentists, anti-socialists, counter-revolutionaries and unpatriotic. *De jure*, a system of self-management gives each individual the right to participate in social, political and economic life, but this constitutional proposition was misused to enable a minority of the political elite to control the population. In this political vacuum, the ruling party elite manipulated fictitious consent. Whenever one of the above-mentioned groups sought to express its discontent, the artificial tranquillity of authoritarian one-party rule was shaken and the ensuing repressive measures were justified by the necessity to enforce law and order to prevent anarchy and chaos in Yugoslav society (Jambrek, 1989).

Before turning to an economic historical analysis of 'the case of Yugoslavia' as a central part of this article, some basic historic and socio-political facts are presented. Finally, the relevance of the 'Yugoslav shipwreck' for Europe's stability, security and development is discussed.

2. Historic roots

The nations comprising Yugoslavia migrated to their present geographic area (homeland) from the area of Asian Russia in a great migration wave in the sixth century. Initially, Croats and Serbs, each separately established tribes in the 'old country', and Montenegrins became the Neretvanian clan. Slovenes were not constituted as a tribe before coming to Europe; they were named Alp Slavs, and consisted of the remains of different Slavic tribes; they mixed into their present area with previous settlers. Hence the big differences between Slovenian dialects today, while such differences are smaller within Croatia or within Serbia. What is true for the Slovenes is true for the Macedonians, while Moslems in Bosnia and Herzegovina were recognized as separate nations only recently.

Previous settlers in the area of Yugoslavia retreated: some to Byzantium in the east, Langobards moved to the west; others, notably the Avars, moved to less populated mountain areas. Later, following the clearing of part of the area by invasions of Turks in the early Middle Ages, Avars came down from the mountains and settled in present-day Albania and Kosovo. Albania was established as a separate state only in 1912 to deprive the Serbs of direct access to the sea.

The Slovenes formed their own state, Karantania, around 1000 BC. The Croats established Greater Croatia (consisting of Dalmatia, Slavonia and Croatia proper) in the tenth and eleventh centuries under King Tomislav. Approximately at the same time, the Serbs created their first independent state in Raška (in the area of present-day Kosovo), under Časlav. After that the Slovenes lost their independence to the Bavarians and later the Croats lost their independence to the Franks. The Serbs first built a strong independent state under Nemanić and Dušan 'The Mighty', which included Macedonia and part of Greece. Bosnia experienced its own statehood under Prince Tvrdko in the fourteenth century before the Turks invaded. Dubrovnik was a separate independent republic in this period, competing with the Venetians for leadership in the Adriatic Sea.

The Turks formed one of the largest Osmanian empires, and from the middle of the fourteenth century started invading the areas of the Southern Slavs. The main consequences were Islamization of the Balkan nations and the second big wave of Slav migration. In their retreat from the Turks the Slavs moved to the west and to the Adriatic coast. The Serbs were moving to present-day Voivodina, and to the Dalmatian coast, where today they remain mixed with Croats.

The Slavs were pagans during their migration from Asia to the Balkans. Here, Slovenes and Croats in the west had been influenced by Roman Christianity, while Serbs and other tribes in the east became Orthodox Christians. While the first two accepted Glagolitic (Latin) handwriting, Serbs and other clans in the east, under the influence of Cyril and Metod, accepted Cyrillic handwriting. In general, the borderline between Western Roman and Eastern Hellenic culture passed through the middle of the Balkans and became especially important after schism in 1054. The eastern South Slavs were ruled by Turks for centuries, while the western region was under German or Hungarian control. From the eighteenth century Slovenes and Croats came under the control of the Habsburgs. Croats were, from the middle of the nineteenth century, under Hungarian authority within the Austro-Hungarian Empire. The Serbs fought two wars for independence from the Turks at the beginning of the nineteenth century and gained internal self-government. Montenegrins achieved a relatively independent status from the Turks, defeating them at the end of the eighteenth century.

The 'Spring of Nations' in 1848 brought a national revival of Slavic nations in the Balkans. National programmes, for the first time, included ideas of a common state entity for all South Slavs. However, while Slovenes and Croats remained in the Austro-Hungarian Empire until its collapse in 1918, Serbia became an independent state after the Berlin Congress in 1978.

The idea of Yugoslavia as a country of all South Slavs was pursued differently in Croatia and Serbia. In the former, an Illyrian state was proposed by Strossmayer and Rački as was an independent Greater Croatia by Starčević. In Serbia, Svetozar Marković proposed the formation of a union of independent nations with equal rights, while Garašanin (1844) proposed the formation of a Greater Serbia. Both plans, of 'Greater Croatia' and 'Greater Serbia', included expansionist aims with respect to other national regions and were the foundation of the nationalist movements of Ustasha (Croats) and Chetnicks (Serbs) during the Second World War.

After the collapse of the Austro-Hungarian Empire, Croats, Slovenes and Serbs who previously belonged to it declared themselves independent states of Croats, Slovenes and Serbs in October 1918, but could not gain international recognition. Being under pressure from aspirants for their land from the west (Italy and Austria), as well as suffering social unrest within their regions, on 1 December 1918 they agreed to join the Kingdom of Serbia and to form, together with Montenegrins (joining Serbia on 25 November 1918), the Kingdom of Serbs, Croats and Slovenes under the Karadjordjević dynasty. Macedonians and Montenegrins were treated as Serbs, while Moslems in Bosnia were not recognized at all. The new monarchy was internationally recognized and, for a time, solved some of the urgent problems of the South Slavs. For the first time in modern history, independence was gained for western South Slav nations. But they were ruled by a Serbian dynasty and thus under Serbian dominance. The rights of all South Slavic nations were not equal, and some nations were not recognized as such at all.

Because of increasing quarrels between nations and the intensifying class struggle, Serbian dominance in the kingdom renamed Yugoslavia - a 'three-headed nation' - increased in the 1930s. Existing nationalist antagonism between Serbs and Croats was used during the Second World War by the conquering Germans, who supported the formation of a 'quisling' independent state of Croatia (under Pavelić) and internal self-government by nationalistic powers in Serbia (under Nedić). Croat Ustasha committed atrocities on Serbs who had moved into their area at the time of the Turkish invasions, while Serb Chetnicks retaliated with atrocities on Croats living in their territory in Bosnia and Herzegovina.

In 1945, Yugoslav partisans, whose struggle for independence had been led by Tito's communists, pursuing a policy of equal treatment and recognition of all South Slav nations, gained overwhelming popular support. Bad memories of nationalist horrors were fresh. 'Communism with a human face' was accepted by a majority of the people because it delivered a better life for them (redistribution of wealth in the 'socialist revolution' increased aggregate welfare; later by increasing the standard of living and fulfilling relatively low starting aspirations, welfare continued to improve).

Continuing improvements in the standard of living and a firm stand against nationalism kept nationalist sentiments under control, and the grip of a one-party political system did not bother Yugoslavs for a while. But, once basic material needs were satisfied and a qualitative step forward was required in the direction of economic efficiency and political democratization in the mid-1960s, the state's leadership was found wanting in courage and wisdom to take such a step. The elite's fear of losing political power together with reborn nationalist aspirations within constituent nations pushed the leadership to reject reforms, inventing a new construct of contractual socialism and economy of associated labour instead. Under their firm grip, national problems had not been solved, merely hidden under the surface. At the same time, satisfactory economic results had been achieved during the 1970s only with the help of external credits. This led to increasing external indebtedness and, after Tito's death, to an inability to repay debts. Yugoslavia found itself in a deep economic and social crisis at the beginning of the 1980s.

Lacking strong cohesive leadership among Tito's successors, and with a decreasing standard of living, conditions were perfect for the resurrection of national(ist) ideas. They became relevant after democratic elections gave way to a multi-party system in all federal units at the end of the 1980s. The winners in the first free elections were anti-communist and pro-nationalist parties. The Yugoslav option did not have a chance in elections even in nationally mixed Bosnia and Herzegovina. Thus communists (under a new name) could win in some republics because they were sufficiently nationalist to take away the nationalist platform from the non-communist opposition. Being unable to deliver a higher standard of living in an economic crisis, the political leadership in the federal units survived only by feeding their people with nationalist slogans (accusing central government and other nations of misusing them).

This is not to say that the introduction of a multi-party system would not have revived national(ist) sentiments that had been artificially suppressed for such a long period. However, had the economic well-being of the people continuously improved, it is just possible that radical nationalist forces would not have gained so much power, and a more civilized way could have been found to solve Yugoslavia's ethnic problems.

The lack of a politically homogeneous leadership with acceptable programmes on the federal level and more than a decade of falling standards of living (negative growth rates, increasing unemployment, inflation and a continuing enormous external debt) meant that the old Yugoslav option was dead, although many in the country and the majority of political powers in the world did not (or did not want to) recognize it. The establishment of the first independent federation of South Slav nations in 1918 fulfilled their long-existing desire for sovereignty, but this solution was 'consummated' at the end of the 1980s. Southern Slavic nations wanted to go a step further to establish their own independent national states (being dissatisfied with the functioning of the Yugoslav federation where each of them, without exception, felt exploited by others). Only after their ultimate goal of establishing national states had been fulfilled might they be able to form economic (and political) associations with other states, giving up willingly a part of their sovereignty they were struggling to retain at the time.

3. Socio-political analysis

The so-called 'Second Yugoslavia' of 1945-91 was a plural society. The well-known slogan said that Yugoslavia was a country with two alphabets, three religions, four languages, five nations and six republics.

The two alphabets were Cyrillic and Latin; the religions were Catholic (32 per cent of the population), Orthodox (41 per cent) and Islamic (22 per cent). The languages were Serbo-Croat (the only cultural factor unifying the majority), Slovene, Macedonian, Albanian; according to the 1981 census the nationalities were Serb (36 per cent of the population), Croat (19.5 per cent), Slovene (7.7 per cent), Montenegrin (less than 2 per cent), Macedonian (7.9 per cent); other citizens - Yugoslav (5 per cent) and those belonging to national minorities (the Albanians among them with a 7.7 per cent share of the Yugoslav population). The dominant ethnic groups in the federal units were the following (with their shares in total population of the unit): Slovenes (92 per cent), Serbs in Serbia proper (85.4 per cent), Albanians in Kosovo (77.4 per cent), Croats (75.1 per cent), Montenegrins (68 per cent) and Macedonians (67 per cent). Only Serbs were dispersed in almost all federal units. Voivodina, Serbia, Bosnia and Herzegovina had heterogeneous populations. Besides economic differences (described later), there was a variation between the federal units in standard of living, life style, family size and other demographic indicators, and culture and political heritage.

Flexibility, necessary for majority democracy in such a plural society, was absent. Under such conditions majority rule was undemocratic and dangerous, because minorities of all kinds were excluded from power and so lost trust in the regime. This led to a majority-rule dictatorship.

A plural society needs a democratic regime based on consensus, which includes rather than excludes. The only potentially viable model for

Yugoslavia could therefore be, following the American political scientist Robert Dahl, a consocionational model, where within (relatively) homogeneous Yugoslav sub-societies and nations representative, competitive, majority democracy (poliarchy) could be developed to degrees.

In the middle of the 1980s *two models* of the political system and culture were developed as a reaction to the deep economic and socio-political crisis in the country. The crisis appeared because of: the death of Tito - the major political integrative power, and the defeat of contractual socialism built on a consensual decision-making process (consensus could never be achieved without coercion in such a heterogeneous country) - and deep economic depression, revealed first by an inability to service external debts at the beginning of the 1980s.

The first model put forward was a monistic one-party democracy or people's democracy, including Serbia (and provinces controlled by Serbia) and Montenegro. This model followed J.S. Mill's concept of a stable competitive democratic order, creating a homogeneous political community (one citizen, one vote, and majority rule).

The second model was a plural parliamentary democracy, introduced first in Slovenia and Croatia, following criteria of human rights and decentralization. The inauguration of this human rights regime required (Jambrek, 1989): application of a majoritarian model of competitive society (Dahl's poliarchy) at the level of relatively homogeneous national territories within Yugoslavia; application of the consensus model of ordered segmentation (Gerald Suttles) or corporate pluralism (Stein Rokkan) at the Yugoslav community level, so that each individual was granted autonomy and could not be permanently deprived by the majority of their rights, freedoms and opportunities.

Applying further Dahl's formula of consocionational societies (for Kosovo and Voivodina as heterogeneous sub-societies) autonomy should have been granted to regions only if a convincing case could be made that the new unit would also meet all the criteria of the democratic process, protecting the minorities in their territories from the tyranny of the majority.

Bosnia and Herzegovina and Macedonia were in their political development somewhere between the two models, trying first to keep (con) federal Yugoslavia alive, but later, during 1991, both coming under pressure from Serbian territorial aspirations and the Serbian quest for political hegemony, moving away from the idea of Yugoslavia under Serbian dominance, proclaiming their sovereignty and trying to find a third way out of the crisis.

It is clear now that the war is over in that all the alternative proposals to save the country in the previous form of federation or even confederation (the EC proposal) are obsolete. Perhaps, if external intervention had come much earlier, at an early stage of internal conflict between the concepts presented above, such proposed solutions to preserve the country intact, could have had a chance. But now federal units under the first model form a new 'narrower' Yugoslavia (greater Serbia with Montenegro, Voivodina,

Kosovo and small regions populated with Serbs in Croatia and Bosnia and Herzegovina), while Slovenia and 'narrower' Croatia have become independent states. Macedonia, Bosnia and Herzegovina followed Slovenia and Croatia to independence, although with enormous and tragic problems.

4. Economic factors
As a centrepiece of this article the economic-historical view includes, first, a general statistical overview of Yugoslav development before and after the Second World War; second, a description of determinants of Yugoslavia's economic collapse; third a presentation of the eventually intolerable economic differences between federal units, and, based on this analysis of properties and changes in economic structure and economic policy, fourth, a description of the development of the economic system (above all labour self-management) and its deficiencies which had an important role in the collapse of the country.

4.1 Indicators of economic and social development, 1918-91
This section will provide statistical evidence to illustrate the development and achievements of Yugoslavia in its life-span. A comparison of the prewar and postwar performance of Yugoslavia is almost absent from literature (due to the lack of comparable statistics); therefore it is given here in some detail. Among statistical sources used are:

Yugoslavia 1918-1988, Federal Statistical Office, Belgrade, 1989
Statistical Yearbook of Yugoslavia 1990, 1991, Federal Statistical Office, Belgrade, 1990, 1991
Statistical reports of The National Bank of Yugoslavia

In summary, the development of Yugoslavia during its life-span was buoyant, partly due to a relatively low starting point, but not constant. Certain lags occurred before the Second World War, decline during the war was significant and the fast progress after the war, accompanied by the well-known socialist cycles, ended in the 1980s. Some figures are as follows:

1. *Area* did not change very much, from 247 to 255.8 thousand square kilometres (with the only gain after the war at the expense of Italy), although the internal institutional structure (borders) changed before the war, but remained unchanged after the war (until the recent 'internal war').
2. *Population* almost doubled in the 73 year life-span of Yugoslavia (the natural rate of growth was 1.58 per cent in 1921, 0.6 per cent in 1981). It numbered 12.545 million people at the first census in 1921 (density around 50 inhabitants per square kilometre), 15.831 million in 1948 and was in 1991 close to 24 million (density around 92 inhabitants per square kilometre). The average age increased from 27.5 years in 1921 (27.9 years for women with a 50.8 per cent share) to 31.0 years in 1981

(34.1 for women with a 50.6 per cent share) and life expectancy was, in 1981, 67 years for men, 74 years for women. The economically active proportion of the population was 50 per cent in 1921, in 1981 only 44 per cent. The rural population in 1921 was 73.3 per cent, in 1948 67.2 percent, but in 1981 19 per cent. These figures indicate one of the fastest transformations from rural to urban society, at least twice as fast as the similar transformation in West European countries. The consequence of this transformation was social instability and unemployment. At the same time, ties of urban population with rural relatives remain strong, thus easing the social and material consequences of unemployment.

3. Large differences in the *natural rate of growth of the population* between federal units occurred despite migration within the country, and emigration, and despite the policy of faster development of the less developed regions because the actual discrepancies between federal units in their level of development never diminished. Thus the natural rate of growth of population in 1950 varied between 2.91 per cent in Kosovo, and over 2 per cent in the other three less developed units (Macedonia, Bosnia and Herzegovina, and Montenegro) and 1.15 per cent in Voivodina, 1.25 per cent in Croatia, 1.26 per cent in Slovenia. In 1987 natural rates were still 2.48 per cent in Kosovo, but only 1.16 per cent in Macedonia (with a large Albanian population), 1.05 per cent in Montenegro and 0.94 per cent in Bosnia and Herzegovina. On the other hand, it was only 0.02 per cent in Voivodina, 0.13 per cent in Croatia, 0.25 per cent in Serbia proper and 0.3 per cent in Slovenia.

4. Thus the differences in 1990 values of *per capita indicators* were: in production 1:7 (Kosovo:Slovenia), in earnings 1:2.5, in social standard 1:2 on average. These persistent differences can be regarded as one of the main economic reasons for the disintegration of Yugoslavia and it is not easy to see what else could have been done to eliminate them in the postwar period. The drive for relative independence in the federal units accompanied by the deficiencies of a self-managed economic system (lack of security for investors from one economic unit into another) did not make direct investments popular. Prevalent indirect investments (the flow of financial credits to the less developed regions), on the other hand, were misused or used inefficiently.

5. There were 25 *nationalities* in Yugoslavia according to the 1981 census (which was conducted in more normal conditions than the last census in 1991). Of Yugoslav citizens 36.3 per cent declared themselves as Serbs, 19.7 per cent as Croats, 8.9 per cent as Muslims, 7.8 per cent as Slovenes, 7.7 per cent as Albanians (their percentage has increased considerably in the last decade), 6 per cent as Macedonians, 5.4 per cent as Yugoslavs (this category almost totally disappeared from the census in 1991), 2.6 per cent as Montenegrins, 1.9 per cent as Hungarians, 0.7 per cent as Gypsies, while the other fifteen nationalities, in total comprising 3 per cent of the population, had shares below 0.5 per cent.

In Croatia 11.5 per cent (530,000) declared themselves as Serbs in 1981. In Slovenia 90.5 per cent declared themselves as Slovenes. In Bosnia and Herzegovina 39.5 per cent were declared Muslims, 32 per cent Serbs and 18.4 per cent Croats. In Montenegro only 3.3 per cent were declared Serbs and in Macedonia 19.7 per cent were declared Albanians.

6. *Religion* is an important element of difference. According to the 1931 census (the last reliable information) among 13.9 million inhabitants 48 per cent were Orthodox Christians, 37.4 per cent were Roman Catholics, 1.7 per cent were Protestant, and 11 per cent Muslims.

7. While in 1920 only 500,000 people (4 per cent of the population) were *employed*, by 1940 that number had doubled, and in 1988 increased to a maximum of 6.884 million people (almost 30 per cent of the population, the remaining important share in the economically active population were private farmers). In 1981, 625,000 Yugoslavs with 250,000 members of their families were temporarily employed abroad. In Yugoslavia only 2.5 per cent were employed in the private sector in 1988, though this share rose thereafter. But, with a large number of registered unemployed (above 1.3 million in 1990 rising to 1.5 million at the end of 1991) the increasing number of lay-offs (the number of employed fell below 6.7 million in 1990 approaching 6.5 million at the end of 1991) from the state sector could not be employed immediately in the emerging private sector. The unemployment rate surpassed 18 per cent in 1991, subsequently approaching the critical limit of 20 per cent. Among the federal units, the *unemployment rate* varied significantly, the main determinants of difference being the level of economic development, demographic expansion and urbanization. Thus, to consider only the extremes, in 1990 the rate of unemployment was only 5.2 per cent in Slovenia (approaching 8 per cent in 1991) and 39 per cent in Kosovo (well above 40 per cent in 1991); 42 per cent of the working population (people between 15 and 65 years old) were employed in Yugoslavia in 1990 (62 per cent in Slovenia, 20 per cent in Kosovo).

8. According to estimations by Stajić the real *national income* increased between 1923 and 1939 by about 50 per cent, reaching US $1158 million in 1939 values (1938 exchange rate $1.00 = 44 dinars), while the population increased by approximately 28 per cent. The per capita national income increased from $62 to $72. In 1947, the national income was approximately US $3 billion, per capita income US $92 in 1972 values. The difference between the 1938 US $ and the 1972 US $ in their purchasing power is relevant for comparison of pre- and postwar Yugoslav national income. The real national income of Yugoslavia increased eight-fold between 1947 and 1989 and as the population increased by 50 per cent, the general standard of living increased in the postwar period four-fold for the average Yugoslav citizen. But, with a very low starting point, relatively fast economic

growth did not diminish Yugoslavia's lag behind developed countries. Thus, according to *The World Bank Atlas 1990*, in 1989 Yugoslavia had a per capita income of $2490 (compared to $14,570 for the UK, for instance).

While in 1923 60 per cent of Yugoslav national income came from primary sectors (agriculture and forestry), 15 per cent from industry and mining and construction, 9.6 per cent from crafts and 12.3 per cent from trade, in 1987 the situation was quite different: 50 per cent came from the secondary sector, only 12 per cent from the primary sector, 4.3 per cent from crafts and the remaining one third from services. As in all socialist countries, the enormous share of manufacturing indicated an out-dated economic structure.

9. *Slovenia*, as the most developed federal unit, had at the beginning of the 1990s 8.5 per cent of the population and 10 per cent of the land, produced around 20 per cent of Yugoslav GNP and had a 30 per cent share in exports (even higher in trade with the hard currency area), but only around a 12 per cent share in the Yugoslav external debt. This illustrates the scale of economic inequalities within Yugoslavia.

10. *Money in circulation* was 3.6 billion dinars in 1920, 17.3 billion dinars in 1940. After the Second World War it had fallen to 3.3 billion dinars in 1952, but increased to 7.786 billion dinars in 1987 and 1,272,414 billion dinars at the end of 1990, 1,719,594 billion dinars in June 1991. With elimination of four zeros at the end of 1989 it was still 172 billion dinars in the middle of 1991.

11. The current *balance of payments* was mostly negative before the war, but outflows were covered at least 80 per cent by inflows and the total export of goods and services counted for no more than 10 per cent of social product on average. Foreign direct investment accumulated to $1.6 billion between 1945 and 1966. With an increasing balance of payments deficit in the 1970s the external debt amounted to $22 billion at the end of 1987 (nearly one-half of yearly GNP), but owing to changes in exchange rates, repayment efforts and swaps the external debt fell to $16 billion at the end of 1990.

12. While *prices* did not increase significantly during the prewar period (during 1927 there was even a decrease on average), after the war, especially from the 1960s on, *inflation* was persistent and rates grew from year to year, achieving a very high level in 1989 (in December 1989 prices rose by 60 per cent). To illustrate the rate of inflation, even with the removal of six zeros, average monthly wages were still in five digits in 1989.

13. *During the Second World War* Yugoslavia lost 1.7 million inhabitants (10.8 per cent of the population). Material damage was $46.9 billion (1938 $ value); direct damage $9.1 billion.

14. In the postwar period *agriculture* increased its production three-fold. Compared to the 1930s plant production was, at the beginning of the 1990s, 2.5 times higher and animal production 3.2 times higher.

Dispersion of land (the size of the average unit) remained substantially unchanged regardless of political changes and war. After the war under socialism, 81 per cent of the land remained privately owned. The area of land devoted to farming increased from 10.7 to 14.1 thousand hectares between 1920 and 1988, although the area of cultivated land after the war stagnated. The quantity of wheat produced increased from 1.363 million tons in 1920 to 3.2 million tons in 1939 and 6.38 million tons in 1988. The production of corn increased similarly. Production of wine doubled compared to the period before the war. The number of cattle stagnated, though pigs more than doubled, horses fell by two thirds, sheep decreased by 30 per cent and poultry increased by 3.5 times. Production of meat, milk and eggs increased three-fold between the prewar period and the late 1980s.

15. Between 1925 and 1987 the area of *forests* increased from 7.0 to 9.4 million hectares (by one-third), the wood mass increased between 1938 and 1979 by 37 per cent. Only one third of all forests remained in private ownership after the Second World War.

16. In 1946, *industrial production* was 20 per cent less than in 1939, but increased 25 times between 1939 and 1989. Production of electricity increased in the same period 70 times, coal production 11 times, crude oil production almost did not exist before the war and reached four million tons in the 1980s; production of cars, non-existent before the war, reached 300,000 vehicles. The number of private *craft* workshops was at the end of the 1980s about the same as before the war (around 160,000), with an additional 1.380 craft-working organizations in social ownership (private workshops employed 274,000 while socially owned shops employed 191.000). Out of seven million apartments around five million were built after the war, one-third of them in the public sector, two-thirds in the private.

17. In *transport* railways did not show any progress after the war. Whereas between 1922 and 1939 the size of the railway system increased by one-quarter, in the next 50 years it remained constant. The number of locomotives and coaches stagnated before the war, but decreased after the war by 20 to 30 per cent. Despite that, the number of passengers and weight of transported goods doubled in the period 1922-39 and doubled (passengers) or quadrupled (goods) in the postwar period. The number of private cars increased from 8000 to 11,500 between 1929 and 1938 and further to 3.3 million in 1989. Similar growth was present for all kinds of road vehicles except motor-bikes, the number of which decreased by one- quarter after 1971 (due to substitution by cars). In the merchant navy, the number of ships in the merchant fleet increased three-fold between 1925 and 1939 and another eight-fold after the war, the number of passengers increased by seven times and transportation of goods by ten times after the war. Air transport increased significantly (from 4 aircraft in 1928 to 50 in 1989, from 1000 to 4 million passengers). The number of telephones increased from 48,000 in 1931

to 62,000 in 1939 to over 4.5 million at the end of the 1980s.

18. In *external trade*, for most of the prewar period the trade balance of Yugoslavia (goods only) was positive; in the postwar period it was negative. At fixed exchange rates exports doubled between 1922 and 1939, but then additionally increased by 100 after the war. *Internal trade* did not have such enormous growth. The number of shops did not increase significantly between 1939 and 1989, but the real volume of trade increased three-fold between 1952 and 1989. The number of wholesale units decreased after the war to one-fifth of the prewar total.

19. The number of private restaurants in 1987 reached only 50 per cent of the prewar 43,000 (because of nationalization under the socialist regime). The number of foreign *tourists* was 205,000 in 1929, 287,000 in 1938, but 9 million in 1988 (domestic 774,000, 720,000 and 12.8 million in the same years). Between 1939 and 1988 the number of border crossings increased by 100 times for foreigners and 200 times for domestic citizens.

20. The last indicators cover developments in the *social* sphere. In *education* the number of primary schools increased by 50 per cent between 1922 and 1939, but then increased by an additional 25 per cent (schools) or 100 per cent (pupils) to late 1980s. In secondary education the number of schools and their pupils increased by two-thirds between 1922 and 1939, while after the war the number of schools increased by an additional 25 per cent, the number of pupils quadrupled. The number of high schools increased from 22 in 1922 to 30 in 1930 and 310 in 1989, while the number of students at the same time increased from 10,000 to 21,000 and then to 350,000.

The number of *theatres* increased from 25 with 3,800 performances and one million spectators in 1933 to 44 with 4200 performances and 1.4 million spectators in 1939 and to 65 with 10,700 performances and 3.2 million spectators in 1987. The number of movie theatres increased from 319 in 1933 to 413 in 1939 and 1250 in 1988 (the maximum number of spectators, 130 million, was achieved in 1960, that is before the TV era in Yugoslavia).

The number of *doctors* increased from 12,000 to 18,000 between 1930 and 1939 and 45,000 in the late 1980s. The number of hospital beds increased from 22,000 in 1930 to 27,000 1938 and 142,000 in the late 1980s.

Only 47,000 persons were *convicted of crimes* in 1927, 110,000 in 1939, 109,000 in 1989.

4.2 The end of Yugoslav economic growth and social development

After the Second World War, a 'New Yugoslavia' started with production and capacity one third below prewar levels and with more than a 10 per cent loss in population. After the conflict with the Soviet Union in 1948, the economy, strongly dependent on trade flows with other East European socialist countries and the Soviet Union, suffered a further fall in production. But, with Western economic help, the newly introduced system of self-management, and orientation to the market economy (within the limits of the socialist system), the second half of the 1950s was a period of the highest economic growth for Yugoslavia - indeed one of the highest growth rates in the world.

After most of the goals of quantitative growth had been achieved in the first half of the 1960s, the economic and social reform introduced in 1965, which should have enabled qualitative steps ahead in the country's development, was rejected by the political leadership because it led to the rise of new centres of power, managers, assumed to be identical or strongly connected to nationalists, expressing their quest for independence in the relatively liberal social environment of the late 1960s. The 'counter-revolution' brought in a new idea of contractual socialism and a contractual economy (as an alternative to the market). The contractual economy as an economic and political system had disastrous economic results which became apparent only in the 1980s. The high economic growth of the 1970s was achieved only thanks to extensive external borrowing. External debts amounted to almost half of the GNP in the early 1980s, at which time a unilateral moratorium on the servicing of debt provoked outside pressure for an economic austerity programme, thus revealing the full scale of the economic crisis with its enormous social implications.

The basic indicators of Yugoslav economic performance in the last twenty years of its existence are given in Table 5.1. It is evident that relatively high growth rates of Gross Social Product (GSP) in 1970 were in effect due to quickly increasing external debt and that in the 1980s there was no more growth. In fact, taking into account net capital outflow in the 1980s (at a yearly rate of approximately 5 per cent of GSP) for debt servicing (in the 1970s Yugoslavia experienced a capital inflow of the same size), the standard of living and welfare (decrease of real wages, increasing unemployment rate, high inflation on the way to hyper-inflation) of the people returned to the levels of twenty years previously.

There were several attempts to stabilize the Yugoslav economy in the 1980s, all bound to be unsuccessful owing to unfavourable external conditions in the first half of the 1980s (high interest rates, high prices of oil and worsening terms of trade) and increasingly unfavourable internal conditions during the 1980s (increased nationalist conflicts, social unrest). The last and the most ambitious attempt was a stabilization programme started by Prime Minister Ante Marković in December 1989. It was wisely described as a 'shock therapy'.

The fact is that at the beginning of his mandate as Prime Minister in 1989, Ante Marković and his cabinet had the support of a relatively large proportion of Yugoslavs. This gave him the chance to win further support for a successful stabilization programme and appropriate reform of the economic system. He was more successful with the latter than with his economic policy decisions. One of his big mistakes was to start Jeffrey Sachs' suggested model of shock therapy, even when the appropriate

Table 5.1 Performance of the Yugoslav economy in 1972-1991(rates of growth in per cent or $billion; official sources)

Year	GSP	IN	PR	BOTC	BOPC	DCD	W	E	OIL
1972	4.3	3.1	16	-0.97	0.42	3.60	0.7	7.0	4.2
1973	4.9	2.2	19	-1.46	0.49	4.27	4.5	8.1	8.3
1974	8.5	9.1	26	-3.43	-1.18	4.77	5.6	9.0	7.4
1975	3.6	9.7	26	-3.59	-1.00	5.89	1.2	10.2	7.4
1976	3.9	8.2	9	-2.48	0.17	7.00	4.5	11.4	8.3
1977	8.0	9.5	13	-3.84	-1.58	8.41	1.9	11.9	9.6
1978	6.9	10.5	13	-4.18	-1.26	10.47	7.3	12.0	10.4
1979	7.0	6.4	22	-6.57	-3.66	13.46	1.7	11.9	11.8
1980	2.3	-5.9	30	5.67	-2.29	17.33	-11.7	11.9	10.9
1981	1.4	-9.8	46	-5.31	-0.75	19.53	- 4.5	11.9	9.4
1982	0.5	-5.5	30	-3.78	-0.46	18.73	- 3.9	12.4	8.5
1983	-1.3	-9.7	38	2.20	-	19.60	-12.1	12.8	9.4
1984	2.0	-9.7	55	-1.70	0.79	19.60	- 5.9	13.3	9.7
1985	0.5	-3.7	77	-1.60	0.27	18.20	3.7	13.8	8.6
1986	3.6	3.5	91	-2.00	0.25	19.20	12.6	14.1	10.8
1987	-1.0	-3.9	118	-1.10	1.10	20.50	- 6.7	13.6	10.9
1988	-1.6	-3.0	199	-0.60	2.20	18.70	- 8.0	14.1	12.1
1989	-2.0	-28.8	1256	-1.50	2.01	17.60	6.2	14.9	11.7
1990	-7.5	-19.0	587	-4.67	-2.66	16.54	-15.8	16.0	13.0
Estimate:									
1991	-15.0	-30.0	75	-3.20	-1.09	17.50	-11.3	18.0	11.0

Key: GSP = gross social product; IN = gross fixed investments; PR = retail prices, yearly averages; BOTC = balance of trade, convertible (in $ billion); BOPC = balance of payments, convertible (in $ billion); DCD = debt to the convertible area (in $ billion); W = real wages; E = rate of unemployment; OIL = import of crude oil (in million tons); 1991 figures are estimates.

framework for its success was absent. This model was relatively success-fully implemented in private economies with well-developed market structures and, either under the control of a totalitarian regime or, alternatively, where general social consensus had been achieved for the realization of the programme in the stabilizing country. Neither precondition existed in Yugoslavia. Therefore it is not surprising that such a programme, after some small success in its transitory period, finally collapsed (increasing inflation, revival of inability to service external debt in 1991). Attempting to implement his own political agenda (the formation of his own political party) Marković accelerated the collapse of the stabilization programme by losing his remaining credibility among the Yugoslav nations. Perhaps, had the economy been in better shape (and had a more appropriate gradual approach with fewer mistakes, which could have been corrected, been adopted), Marković's cabinet might have had a chance to retain enough credibility among Yugoslavs to have been able to conduct a peaceful transformation of the 'Second Yugoslavia'.

4.3 Economic disparities between federal units

The economic and demographic disparities between the Yugoslav federal units were enormous. The ratio between Slovenia and Kosovo as extreme cases was 7:1 in GNP per capita and 1:10 in population natural growth rate. The relevant conclusion is that merely to retain the absolute distance between the two, in the case of further moderate growth of GNP per capita in Slovenia, Kosovo needed a substantial GNP growth rate above all realistic limits. Despite redistribution of income and permanent reallocation of resources (through three sources: a federal fund for less developed regions in which all units participated with 1.5 to 2 per cent of their GNP; subventions through the federal budget, about a quarter of which was intended for these purposes; and direct credits from the central bank), which enabled most indicators of social standard and wages difference not to exceed 1:3, differences in their level of economic development (above all, in productivity) did not decrease during the entire forty-five years of postwar Yugoslavia. Under these circumstances, it must be counted a success that they did not increase substantially.

For the sake of impartiality, it must be emphasized that the relatively closed (high import taxes) market system, with strong restrictions on primary commodities markets, helped producers of final goods in the more developed federal units by giving them relatively favourable terms of trade. To conclude, there is no way to calculate who exploited whom in the country. It is not surprising that at the end all the federal units claimed to be exploited.

Table 5.2 illustrates some of the late differences between Yugoslav federal units. According to data from Yugoslav official sources Montenegro's economy was the most open to the world (tourism, transport), while Macedonian and Serbian provinces were the least. Montenegro had the largest share of sales to other federal units, followed by Voivodina (agriculture), Serbia and Macedonia. The least connected with the rest of Yugoslavia were Croatia, Kosovo, Slovenia and Bosnia and Herzegovina. According to the World Bank criteria, only Kosovo was severely externally indebted; moderately indebted were Serbia, Bosnia and Herzegovina, Macedonia and Montenegro, while Voivodina, Croatia and especially Slovenia were only lightly indebted.

Differences in the natural growth of population were, and are, enormous, from negative growth in Voivodina to an explosion in Kosovo. Unemployment rates also differed significantly. They were positively correlated with the growth of population and negatively with the level of economic development. For federal units with unemployment rates over 20 per cent and for Kosovo with 38.8 per cent at the beginning of the 1990s it is clear there was a socially explosive situation. The comparison of average nominal wages and GNP per capita for federal units (in both cases Yugoslavia is taken as 100) shows a significant redistribution process: federal units with the lowest GNP per capita had relatively higher wages than their production merited (notably Kosovo, Bosnia and Herzegovina, Macedonia and vice versa for federal units with the highest GNP per capita (Slovenia, Voivodina, Croatia).

Table 5.2 Differences between Yugoslav federal units: selected economic, demographic and social indicators

Indicator	BIH	MON	CRO	MAC	SLO	SERt	SERp	KOS	VOI
Social product in 1990, YU = $53.2 billion (Share in YU, %)									
	12.4	1.8	25.6	5.4	19.6	35.2	22.5	1.9	10.9
Convertible export of goods and services, 1990 (in $ million)									
	2157	640	6533	652	4904	5344	3864	220	1260
Openness of the economy 1990 (Export/Product)									
	0.33	0.67	0.48	0.23	0.47	0.29	0.32	0.22	0.22
Convertible external debt, September 1990 (in $ million)									
	1677	597	2994	761	1788	4869	3302	726	841
Sales to other federal units as % of final demand									
	37.4	48.5	34.0	41.9	36.8	42.4	41.2	34.6	46.8
Population in 1990 (million)									
	4.5	0.6	4.7	2.1	1.9	9.8	5.8	2.0	2.0
Rate of natural growth of population, 1990 (per 1000)									
	7.7	8.9	0.5	9.9	2.5	5.1	1.4	23.1	-1.6
Unemployment rate, 1990 (in %)									
	21.1	22.2	9.0	23.0	5.2	19.5	16.7	38.8	17.1
Average nominal wages, 1990 (YU = 100)									
	80	74	114	76	136	93	96	53	97
GNP per capita, 1989 (YU = 100)									
	65	71	123	65	200	88	100	24	118
Cost of living index, 1989-90 (in %)									
	675	707	694	697	652	678	686	705	669
Average yearly GNP growth rate, 1970-89 (in %)									
	3.5	3.4	3.1	3.6	3.6	3.4	3.5	3.6	3.1
Average Yearly Employment Growth Rate, 1970-1989 (in %)									
	4.1	4.2	2.7	4.0	2.3	3.0	3.1	4.9	2.4
Social capital per worker, 1988 (YU = 100)									
	93	137	110	74	137	87	82	89	101
Persons per doctor, 1989									
	572	542	383	398	373	400	335	868	405

Key: BIH=Bosnia and Herzegovina, MON=Montenegro, CRO=Croatia, MAC=Macedonia, SLO=Slovenia, SERt=Serbia total, SERp=Serbia proper, KOS=Kosovo, VOI=Voivodina

Differences in the cost of living index for 1989-1990 were not very large, but they existed. They were positively correlated with the amount by which nominal wages exceeded GNP per capita, so that they corrected to a certain extent the redistribution in wage rates.

Differences between federal units in average yearly GNP growth rates in the last twenty years were small (values between 3.1 per cent and 3.6 per cent yearly), while differences in employment growth rates were larger (values between 2.3 per cent and 4.9 per cent). Comparing both enables a conclusion to be drawn about trends in labour productivity in federal units: they were positive only in Slovenia, Croatia, Voivodina and Serbia and highly negative in Kosovo. Differences in the amount of social capital at the disposal of workers were relatively small (with respect to differences in product per worker). Social indicators (number of persons per doctor) differed the most within Serbia total(!), namely between Serbia proper with only 335 persons and Kosovo with 868 persons. Not only this, some other indicators show that disparities within some of the federal units were also significant.

Given only selected economic, demographic and social indicators, it becomes clear why Yugoslavia was too heterogeneous a country to be able to exist without permanent internal conflicts and rivalry.

4.4 Was workers' self-management a viable alternative to the communist and capitalist economic systems?

Prewar Yugoslavia had a capitalist economic system. It was among the least developed European countries, with heavy emphasis on agriculture, and a country whose institutions of modern industrial capitalism (for example a stock exchange, financial institutions and instruments) were less developed. Certain political changes in the system in the direction of higher centralization in the 1930s did not change the basic nature of the system.

After the Second World War Yugoslavia introduced a socialist political system and with it frequent changes in the economic system. The cynic might be excused for attributing the over-production of legal and constitutional documents to attempts to compensate for the chronic inefficiency of the socialist system in practice

With regard to development of the postwar economic system of Yugoslavia, four periods can be identified, following closely major constitutional changes. They are:

1. Administrative central planning socialism (1945-53)
2. Administrative self-managed socialism (1953-63)
3. Self-managed market socialism (1963-74)
4. Contractual self-managed socialism (1974-90)

The first system after the Second World War was a close copy of the 'real socialist' system of the Soviet Union (similar to other East European countries). Conflict with the Soviet Union (Informbiro, 1948) was a cause and consequence of the new invention: self-management.

In the 1950s self-management was first introduced in the economy, and later in all other sectors of social life. In the beginning the new system stimulated the engagement of working people, and their modest aspirations were quickly fulfilled. This was the period of Yugoslavia's fastest economic growth.

With the attainment of a certain level of economic (and social) development, when basic economic needs were satisfied, a further qualitative step was needed. The economic and social reforms of 1965 were an attempt in the direction of liberalization of the economic sphere (featuring the introduction of the market mechanism on a larger scale including the elements of labour and the capital market) as well as the social sphere (decentralization of political life with national autonomy emphasized, though still within a one-party political framework). The undesired consequences of a functioning market mechanism in the economy (enlarged income differences according to individuals' abilities) and in political life (leading to a multi-party system), where the party elite was losing power to independent managers and national(ist) forces, led Tito's leadership to put an end to the reform process.

Instead of a market with its 'undesired, uncontrollable powers' the leadership invented a substitute for it, a third way to plan the market, called the 'social agreement'. In this system, the 'chaotic forces of the market' could be replaced by controlled agreements between agents in the economic as well as the social spheres, including politics. The idea of millions of contracts and agreements controlling the economic and social life of Yugoslavia was a pervasive idealistic fantasy, imposed on everyday life without a real chance to succeed. The third way proved to be no way at all.

Can the same be said of the whole idea of self-management, based on the Yugoslav experience? Here, the answer should be more qualified. In its mature stage the Yugoslav economic system of workers' self-management was based on four basic elements: social ownership of the means of production, workers' self-management in economic units, market and income relations. These foundations were inconsistent both with each other and internally so that they could not lead to the optimal performance of the economy.

(a) *Social ownership of means of production* (neither private nor state) remained an undefined concept, which allowed misuse of resources in practice. As ownership rights are usually executed in the form of denying others the use of the object one owns, if all society is the owner, there is nobody to be excluded within the country (Štiblar, 1991). As a consequence, the popular definition said that social ownership was ownership by everybody and nobody. It was no surprise that certain individuals (usually in higher political positions) used this 'everybody's property' in his/her own interest without material responsibilities for the consequences of misuse.

(b) *Self-management* means direct individual participation in the decision-making process of economic units. But, when there is a large number of complex decisions to be made, there is not enough time nor enough knowledge among workers. The result was that people worked effectively less than four hours per day and that many decisions that were rightly the responsibility of professionals (technological, marketing, managerial) were formally transferred to workers' councils, thus leaving workers to take material responsibility for the consequences of such decisions. While external political leadership or internal management imposed solutions, workers were responsible for their quality. In the common event of mistakes, external political power gave help to bail out unsuccessful enterprises, thus forming an unusual symbiosis between workers and managers. One of the proposed corrections of the system was that workers should vote only once a year by secret ballot on the maintenance of the mandate of management in the factory, taking into account only earnings and their material status, and leaving all other professional matters to the management, which was qualified and should be responsible for such decisions (Bajt, 1990). Extensive inclusion of social security criteria in the economy softened the budget constraints of economic units, thus opening the way to the moral hazard problem and, as a final consequence, to inefficiency.

(c) *The market system* is inconsistent with self-management with regard to the market of factors, capital and labour. A worker cannot simultaneously fulfil the role of labourer and owner. Social capital cannot be sold, so a capital market cannot exist. Further, the constitutional requirement was that social capital could not be decreased in the process of production. Although it meant a proposition against stealing social property, it meant that losses, a regular event in a market economy, could not be recognized as such. In such an environment the criteria of efficient production were invisible and disregarded.

(d) *Income relations* were formulated with a provision that everyone was paid according to his/her work, not according to needs (a proposition of Communism). But, there were problems in introducing this proposition into real life, as it led to enormous social-economic differentiation, unacceptable to the leadership (following Lenin's assertion that market forces enable differentiation between workers' earnings, thus transforming socialism into capitalism). Therefore, the division of wages according to work (not only done, but as evaluated in the market) was never fully realized, thus destroying an important stimulus to efficient work and management of the economy, leaving it inferior to the capitalist systems in that sense. *Ex-post* correction of income distribution with a tax system (in the social-democratic spirit) was never considered or applied as an alternative.

Certain unrealistic assumptions about the qualities of individual human beings have to be made for the self-management system described to function properly (in a socially just and economically efficient manner) in real life. An ideal individual, living in this system, should be:

(i)   altruistic (not egoistic) human beings who prefer common well-being to their own (and that of their family);

(ii)   omnipotent, equally qualified for all professions and jobs;

(iii) one with infinite time at his/her disposal for (originally direct, not through delegates) participation in discussions and decision-making processes at work, in his/her home district and in different interest associations including politics, local and national;

(iv) someone deriving satisfaction more from non-material goods than from material goods.

Even if allowance is made for exaggerations of the qualities required for an individual living in the Yugoslav self-managed system, one can still conclude that such an ideal human being does not exist today and that forty years of re-education did almost nothing to create such individuals in Yugoslavia. As with the idea of communism in general, self-management in the Yugoslav forms is a system meant for a society of material abundance, high technology (with ample free time for the individual) and which has solved all other conflicts of interest (such as national tensions, for instance). It is clear that most developed societies today would be more appropriate for such a self-managed system (similar to the unfulfilled prediction of Marx and Engels for communism), but even they, with their level of development, are light-years away from it. This was even more true then for the people of underdeveloped Yugoslavia. This is not to assert that self-managed market socialism ('socialism with a human face' as it was sometimes described in Czechoslovakia in 1968) is not substantially different from hard-core Stalinist 'real' socialism (communism), but only that preconditions for its efficient application are far from being fulfilled in today's world. At the same time, in contrast to 'real' socialism, some ideas and solutions from the self-managed economic system could be taken over, and they do actually flourish in certain forms of workers' participation in the decision-making process in the West (for instance, German partnership, American ESOPs, certain rights of British trade unions, the Netherlands' worker participation and certain self-government solutions at the local community level).

5. Europe and the Yugoslav question

In historic perspective Yugoslavia was a product of decisions made by the Allies in Western Europe and the USA after the First World War, and the status of 'Second Yugoslavia' was guaranteed in peace conferences after the Second World War. Previously and later in history, Yugoslavia, and the nations which were included in Yugoslavia, were the subject of manipulation and of special interests of neighbouring European countries. But Yugoslavia was always dealt with 'by the way', with insufficient understanding and lack of interest in, and knowledge of, the problems of South Slavic and other nations and nationalities living in the Balkans. Because the interests of countries involved in drawing up the settlements have always taken priority, outside interventions have rarely been appropriate or successful. On the other hand, being burdened with all the differences described above, the nations comprising Yugoslavia have never been able to solve their disputes by themselves. Thus the Balkans, and especially Yugoslavia, were correctly named the powder-keg of Europe. That is an exact description of what has happened since the middle of 1991 in Yugoslavia: the powder-keg exploded.

After the Second World War Western Europe (and the USA) embraced Yugoslavia, supporting it in its conflict with the Soviet Union, giving economic help but then stopping short of helping the country to reform the democratic Western-European way. Yugoslavia was never a part of Europe in the eyes of the Western Europeans. It was a typical case of marginalization. The country had a relatively better position in other international institutions (notably the World Bank and the IMF).

Some help was given by Western Europe in the form of the Agreement *sui generis* between the European Union (EU) and Yugoslavia in 1981 (if fully realized it should have brought Yugoslavia around $500 million per year, but it was never fully realized and help of less than 1 per cent GNP per year is not very significant). Also, an agreement of co-operation was reached between EFTA and Yugoslavia (the Bergen Declaration of 1984), though without effective economic and/or social consequences. Yugoslavia was never accepted in the Council of Europe, when such membership would have eased the process of solving its internal disputes.

If the EU becomes a fortress of Europe, as some people fear, access by non-EU countries to its markets will be much more difficult. The trade diversion effect will have negative consequences for the nations of ex-Yugoslavia. For the new states it will mean worsening terms of trade, decreasing production and employment. Advantages of the economy of scale for EU members will at the same time become disadvantages to marginal European countries like the new states on the territory of former Yugoslavia. In October 1991, a contract was signed between the EU and EFTA, under which a new European Economic Area (EEA) was formed. This constituted a new step toward economic improvement for its members and an additional step back for the other countries in Europe, like the post-Yugoslav states, which are not its members.

As a member of the European Economic Area and not on its margin, Yugoslavia, probably, would not have been such a difficult problem to solve. There would have been a legal basis for outside intervention (or intermediation even before conflict turned into war). Proposed and attempted economic sanctions were ineffective in the short run and were unable to stop the war. They affected, above all, the general population and not the army and warring factions.

Western Europe (with the rest of the world) had to engage itself fully in the process of the solution of the crisis of former Yugoslavia. Not because of altruism, but for selfish reasons, Europe needs peace and security on its margins. It is clear that reforming Eastern Europe and the disintegrated Soviet Union will for a long period to come be a source of instability (economic, national and social). The appropriate approach to solve the ex-Yugoslav crisis (bolstering self-determined independence for every nation, preserving peace with military surveillance, a selective approach to new states taking into account their respective levels of democratization, and economic aid) could be taken as an example for the solution of similar (maybe not so acute) problems in other countries in Europe, constructed as unnatural federations which will, no doubt, appear in the near future.

The author wishes to state that the final version of this paper was written in 1993 and only slightly amended in 1996.

Bibliography

Bajt, A. (1990), *Samoupravna oblika družbene lastnine*. Globus, Zagreb.

Jambrek, P. (1989), 'Human Rights in Multiethnic State: The Case of Yugoslavia', mimeograph, Pravna fakulteta Ljubljana, p. 1-36

Mrak, M. (ed.), (1990), *Financial System and Policies in Yugoslavia*. Report for UNCTAD, Ljubljana, p. 1-101.

Odlok o skupnih ciljih monetarne politike in projekcija plačilne bilance, SIV, Belgrade, 1991.

Statistički godišnjak Jugoslavije 1990, Belgrade.

Štiblar, F. (1991), *Federal Units in Yugoslavia*. Report to EC Directorate, WIIW. Vienna, p. 1-10.

Štiblar, F. (1991), *External Indebtedness of Yugoslavia and its Federal Units*, WIIW. Forschungsberichte No. 175. Vienna, p. 1-22.

Yugoslavia, Statistical Survey No. 5. NBY, Belgrade 1991.

Yugoslavia, 1918-1988. Savezni statistički zavod. Belgrade, 1989.

Zgodovina 1-4, *Državna založba Slovenije*, 1983-1990. Ljubljana

CHAPTER SIX

Transformation and the Legacy of Backwardness: Thoughts from a Romanian Perspective

Daniel Daianu

1. Transition: new and old connotations

It is not unfair to say that the post-communist transition in Central and Eastern Europe and in what was the Soviet Union is the hottest theoretical and policy-related topic among economists and other social scientists today. Transition, understood as 'transformation'[1] of the command economy into a market-based system, or 'the economics of transition' dominates much of the academic discourse and of the work of specialized international bodies like the International Monetary Fund and the World Bank. Prestigious economists[2] from leading universities of the world jumped on the bandwagon of history, seeing a unique opportunity for taking part in grand-scale institutional engineering, for what is at stake - in post-communist societies - is the creation of viable economic entities by means, essentially, of institutional (systemic) reconstruction.

If the system-related (institutional) dimension of transition is of paramount importance, one can also detect another meaning which crosses ideological borders and has defined the evolution of these societies throughout this century, the quest for catching up with the West, an idea which obsessed national politicians during the interwar period, communist leaderships bent on proving the alleged superiority of their system, and which, today, is reflected in the ardent desire to join the European Union. For example, in pre-communist Romania both the Liberal Party and the Peasant Party wanted to get the country away from her economically peripheral position in Europe; to this end they propounded different policies. The Liberals favoured protection of industry and state involvement in the economy, thinking more in terms of what one today would call dynamic comparative advantages and strategic industrial policy,[3] and feared foreign encroachment in the emerging Romanian industrial sectors and the marginalization of the national entrepreneurial class. The Peasants espoused an 'open door' policy.[4] This conceptual and policy divide was not uncommon in the region at that time and was made more clear by the consequences of the Great Depression. The Romanian communist leadership viewed the catching-up issue in relation to both the capitalist countries and the more advanced economies of the Moscow-led bloc. The industrialization drive in the postwar period was justified not only in ideological terms, but was also linked to national assertiveness among fellow communist countries in particular, and among the other nations of the world in general. It is ironic, then, that part of the particularly difficult legacy of communism in Romania is attributable to the effects of her self-imposed insulation from the winds of institutional change and reforms which were blowing in some neighbouring countries after 1956. This anti-reformist stance made it impossible for the national environment to evolve into something closer to the transformation of the 1990s and it encouraged a sequence of irrational industrial policy choices which ran counter to the stated ultimate goal of reducing development gaps. It is striking that in post-communist Romania the debate on how to integrate faster into the European economic space evinces an underlying concern with the country's image in the West, and its failings when compared to the standing of Hungary, Poland and the Czech and Slovak Republics. There is no doubt that Romania's poorer image can be directly linked with its track record of pre-revolutionary failure to reform under local communism, which can be characterized as a result of a scarcity of market ingredients. Later on I shall return to this issue when talking about the economics of transition as applied to 'front-runners' as against 'laggards'. By the latter I mean countries like Romania, Bulgaria and the former Soviet republics, which did not attempt reform before 'the Big Bang' of 1989.

Why do I emphasize this quest for catching up? Because frequently one sees allegedly knowledgeable professionals making judgements on the transformation process while seeming oblivious to the heavy legacy of backwardness of these societies, a state of affairs which goes back deeply into history.[5] As a keen student of the area has remarked, '... Eastern Europe was in some sense economically backward long before it was absorbed into the broader Western world market. This backwardness has roots in the very distant past ...'. (Chirot, D.1989, p. 3). Backwardness should be seen as bearing considerably on the potential for overcoming the performance deficit of institutionally poorly arranged societies; it points, on the one hand, to the lack of knowledge of individuals and of society as a whole and to the constraints on institutional change and, on the other hand, it suggests that there is much scope for a system to deviate from what could be conceived as an ideal 'corridor'[6] of evolution (which involves and is dependent on institutional reconstruction or, as in the case of post-communist societies, system transformation, I remember in this respect how baffled were some of my Romanian colleagues when Ken Jowitt, a political scientist from Berkeley and an astute observer of my country, said that, 'Latin American countries have been in transition for more than a century'.[7] He was referring not only to mistaken economic policies (Argentina comes immediately to mind for it belonged to the group of advanced economies - in terms of per capita income - before the Second World War), but also to institutional bottlenecks rooted in a certain level of development.

My stress on the legacy of backwardness is not meant to diminish in any way the importance of institutional reconstruction; it aims, none the less, to point up the dragging effects of this legacy and the unfavourable path of dependency which is not easy to break away from. Against this background, the relationship between the economic system of communism and the legacy of backwardness (for the post-communist societies) can be the object of further analytical scrutiny. Czechoslovakia - a leading industrial economy in interwar Europe - provides a conspicuous example of the negative impact of the command system on the performance of the economy. This performance deficit can be judged in both static and dynamic terms: statically, as the distance from a level of output resulting from a full and efficient utilization of resources (which presupposes adequate institutional arrangements); and dynamically, as the damage caused over time to the quality (performance potential) and quantity of the factors of production, as well as the lack of viability of the economic system - doomed to fail because of its inner laws of motion.

The command system has a logic of self-destruction, prophetically anticipated by L. von Mises and Fr. von Hayek in the much-celebrated Calculation debate, which finds only a partial explanation in the process of institutional obsolescence (decay) and fading away of an 'all encompassing interest', (Olson andMurrell, 1991). Communism, despite its aberrant nature, brought about huge social mobility and turned predominantly agrarian societies (with the exception of Czechoslovakia and the former East Germany) into semi-industrial societies with most of the active workforce consisting of industrial workers;[8] it practically eliminated illiteracy, and contributed decisively to the secularization of these societies.[9] This endeavour to modernize, which was accompanied by terror and violence as state policy (forced collectivization is a telling example) could not alter the logic of the historical demise of the system; moreover, it sowed new seeds of social, political and economic decomposition. Outbursts like those of 1953 in the former East Germany, 1956 in Hungary and Poland, 1968 in Czechoslovakia, 1970, 1976 and 1980 in Poland and 1977 in Romania are proof of how the population felt about the nature of the system. The fact remains that at the end of the 80s - in spite of the high literacy rate of the population and of highly skilled segments of the labour force - Central and Eastern Europe appeared as falling increasingly behind the developed market economies, unable to compete with even developing market economies (the newly industrializing countries in particular), possessing oversized and growingly obsolete industrial facilities and projecting the image of a looming ecological disaster.

How does the cultural factor fit in the whole picture? - after all, backwardness has a cultural dimension. It is obvious that transformation and, in a broader sense, catching up with the West implies cultural change as well. I pinpoint two features which seem relevant.

One is linked with historical and cultural differences between the Western world and the whole, or part, of Central and Eastern Europe.[10] The other aspect regards the cultural legacy of communism, an ethos which shaped the behaviour and expectations of large masses of people and still plays havoc with transformation as an intended process or strategy. A further question can be raised as to what extent the cultural peculiarities which preceded communism and its cultural legacy constrain the process of transformation and demand adaptations of the new institutional arrangements. The question can be formulated thus: which western economic model best fits the area?[11]

The challenges facing the post-communist leaders are enormous, nearly overwhelming if one realizes that progress is being pursued simultaneously on several tracks: creating viable (market-based) economic entities, setting up pluralist democratic polities, re-entering a path of economic growth and achieving modernization (including cultural change). Since transformation as a real process cannot be decoupled from its concrete context, which itself is the product of both remote and recent history, I will deal with specifics of the evolution of the Romanian economy under communism.

2. The grand failure in Romania

Seeking legitimacy at home and espousing a specific brand of economic nationalism,[12] the communist leaders of Romania - Ceausescu in particular - strove to turn Romania into an industrial stronghold; forced industrialization, hyper-centralization of decision-making and the shunning of the 'socialist international division of labour' were crucial components of the strategy of economic policy over the whole period of communist rule. The outcome is well-known; in addition to all that defines any command economy Romania ended up with an overdiversified, oversized and technologically obsolete industrial sector, huge imbalances between economic sectors, a ruined agriculture and one of the lowest living standards in Europe. Most of these features sound familiar but they were predominant even when comparing Romania to other nations in the former communist bloc.

Bearing in mind the purpose of this paper,[13] it would be redundant to produce an overview of the economic history of the last forty years, all I wish to do is point out several aspects which made Romania's experience 'remarkable' and which can shed light on some developmental matters and help explain the peculiar economic situation of the country in December 1989.

Romania under communism stands out for its unflinching adherence to Stalinist precepts of economic policy: its isolationism, its industrial policy choices which blatantly ignored the reality of comparative advantages, its trade policy choices that ran counter to the very logic of functioning of the domestic economy and a *sui generis* 'shock therapy' in the 190s. If asked to put this abysmal record into a conceptual nutshell, I would link the performance deficit of the economic entity to its mode of functioning (the set of institutional arrangements),[14] its economic policy, and the surrounding environment.[15] On all these accounts Romanian policy-makers fared miserably.

At the end of the 1980s the Romanian economy was the most centralized in the former Soviet-led bloc. The history of reforms in communist Romania is, comparatively, an almost blank sheet; what was attempted in 1967 and 1978 aborted quickly, owing either to the political frailty of those championing real change[16] or the lack of genuine intentions.[17] What were some of the main consequences of this stunning rigidity and ideological immobilism? I would mention, first, the relative scarcity of market ingredients,[18] which found expression in the lack of institutional prerequisites for the easing of the transformation of the system and the lack of a business culture (embodied by an entrepreneurial class). Obviously, the economic doctrine of the Party and, related to it the mode of functioning of the economy (with extreme centralization of power and no checks and balances) made possible Romania's uniquely arbitrary economic and industrial policy, with its near-total disregard for factors of production and ability to compete in world markets. It is obvious that the mode of functioning of the economy (the economic mechanism) is essential in explaining its performance; what I believe still needs to be stressed is the damage caused to the economy in a dynamic sense, to its performance *potential*. Institutional rearrangements (turning the system into a market-based economy) could not lead to that increase of performance which might be suggested by past flows of inputs (accumulated capital and human stock) and macrostructural changes. One should recall that Romanian communist leaders boasted frequently about the 'statistical' achievements of the economy; they liked to talk about a 'Romanian economic miracle' and sought to emulate East Asian growth rates. To this end they forced the pace of accumulation in the 1960s and 1970s.[19]

The Stalinist model was also fatal for the 'turning away from the CMEA' orientation that was initiated in the 1960s.[20] Functionally extremely rigid, protectionist and increasingly unreliable owing to its growing complexity,[21] the Romanian economy could not capitalize on the opportunities arising from the attempt to extricate itself from the trade diversion and efficiency effects of the CMEA. This orientation to world markets was doomed to failure because of an inappropriate domestic base and a lack of supporting internal markets. What Japan, South Korea, Taiwan, or Singapore could achieve was out of reach of a command economy of the worst sort; the highly interventionist policies of the East Asian governments (less marked in Taiwan, though significant even there) does not change the fundamental truth that theirs are essentially market economies.

Though the mode of functioning of the economy predetermines the nature of and the realm of choices for economic policy, policy-makers have substantial opportunity to influence policy outcomes. A command economy, as a supply-constrained system, reproduces shortages on a steady basis, but the size of imbalances depends on what planners do; they can, for example, pay more or less attention to the comparative advantages of the country, even when the irrationality of domestic prices obscures them. The scope for major blunders in economic policy is immense under command planning, and Romania provides ample evidence in this regard. For example, the former communist countries face dissimilar energy and food problems. Amazingly, Romania, which used to be the granary of the sub-region and has huge potential in agriculture and a considerable natural resources base (compared to her neighbours) had a very precarious food situation for many years and became heavily dependent on foreign sources for raw materials and energy. One could argue that such a dependency should not be necessarily of concern: this is perfectly true if the economy is running efficiently. But Romania is not like Japan, where imported input goes into the 'black box' of the economy and comes out as a high value-added output with a high likelihood of being an exportable good.

Romania provides an interesting and instructive case of 'immiserizing growth' caused by the logic of the system - by the rush to speed up industrial growth[22] and to increase ties with market economies on a weak functional basis. In the literature this phenomenon is explained by the existence of various price distortions which harm resource allocation, worsen the terms of trade and lower the welfare level.[23] But one should regard the very mode of functioning of the economy (including the implementation of wrong industrial choices) as the fundamental distortion which leads to immiserizing growth. It can be shown that the inner dynamics of the system - its incapacity to cope with increasing complexity and inability to assimilate and generate technological progress - lead to a 'softening' of output, towards expansion with a heavy bias towards industrial soft goods, which in turn leads to a steady deterioration of the terms of trade. This is what happened in Romania where forced industrialization gave precedence to steel, chemical and machine-building industries, and agriculture was terribly squeezed. The unhealthy nature of such growth can be explained succinctly. The biased expansion towards the production of soft goods undermines the comparative advantages of the economy and demands a quantity of hard inputs which could either be provided only by disrupting domestic production, or not be achieved at all - for many export-destined goods were unsaleable.[24] Actual exports of soft goods are hence smaller than the level programmed and the remaining necessary inputs are obtained through an international exchange of hard goods. This means that the country has to forgo the consumption of certain kinds of hard goods (notably consumer goods, which were in high demand from ordinary citizens) in favour of acquiring other types of hard goods, such as energy, raw materials and spare parts; the welfare loss for the population is tremendous and it, in turn, triggers a supply-multiplier on the part of consumers in their role of labour suppliers. Apart from the fatal consequences of having been embedded in, and the product of, a non-market environment the strategy of industrialization in Romania (and in the other command systems as well) teaches several lessons:

1. A development programme must be based on a realistic assessment of the economy's capabilities and potential.
2. Technological and economic possibilities are constrained by the overall development level of the economy; these bounds cannot be pushed outwards limitlessly by capital and technology imports.
3. There is a 'speed limit' for the pace of improvement in the technological sophistication of productive apparatus, which is determined by the 'learning curve' of labour, the stock of managerial resources and the qualitative structure of factors of production. This speed limit suggests that there is an objective to go through successive stages (or processing levels) in the industrialization process.
4. Meeting the basic needs of the population is a must for both social and economic reasons. When consumers' preferences are grossly neglected

labour dissatisfaction and contraction (the labour supply multiplier,[25] which operates both quantitatively and qualitatively) has grave repercussions.

5. When a country is poor it does not make sense 'to put up with the burden of preventable waste that arises even within the static framework of given wants, techniques and resources', (Myint, 1971, p. 16). Support given to agriculture and to the development of infrastructure, and the stimulation of entrepreneurship (which means not emasculating market forces) are essential ingredients in a self-sustained growth process.

6. For less developed economies, with a supposedly low innovative capacity, static factors (the cost of labour and raw material procurement) are basic for making good use of comparative advantages. The higher the procurement cost of primary resources, the higher must be the processing level of goods in order to compensate for the loss in terms of the 'static production function' and, therefore, the smaller the chance that an economy that does not innovate and evinces a hard goods supply constraint (like the command economies) can be competitive.

7. By combining static and dynamic time perspectives one can speak of an ideal (optimal) sequence of stages of climbing up the ladder of development which would minimize the costs of catching-up over a given period of time.[26]

Returning to factual history, the start of the 1980s highlighted Romania's grand economic failure; external shocks (like the rise in the oil price or the sharp increase in world real interest rates), which were mitigated only for a short time by external financing, accelerated the decline of the economy. Ceausescu rejected any suggestion of market-inspired reforms that could have improved the performance of the economy and its export capacity. In order to cope with the burden of debt repayments, he commanded an unprecedented (literally unprecedented in the history of the world) policy of paying back the entire external debt as soon as possible by means of its 'internalization' (Daianu, 1984). He succeeded in enforcing this extraordinary 'shock therapy' by means of a dramatic squeeze on domestic absorption; there was a substantial drop in consumption, and long-term growth possibilities were impaired by an unusual curtailment of imports of machinery and equipment from Western countries.[27] This policy relied on a strengthening of the country's isolation and the suppression of any dissenting views.

At the end of the 1980s, the Romanian economy, the country and the people presented a desolate image. After more than four decades of forced industrialization, the competitiveness of the economy was at the bottom of the communist league, disequilibria among sectors and shortages were increasing, the people's plight was beyond imagination;[28] the country was imploding. Romania was a laggard among her neighbours in terms of institutional prerequisites for the post-communist transition; there was little psychological preparedness in the population for abrupt change, and almost no social base for market reforms. Moreover, the 'shock therapy' of the 1980s had created very high expectations for an immediate and substantial improvement of material conditions after a change of ruler (or of regime), which presaged a high degree of intolerance for new austerity measures. The legacy of Romanian communism was a unique economic and institutional backwardness which has seriously affected Romania's post-communist transition.

3. On the economics of transition: front-runners vs laggards

The early euphoria and high expectations of the chain reaction collapse of communist regimes have been replaced by sobriety, caution and anxiety. Both professionals and laymen realize that the process of transformation is much more complex than was initially anticipated. For example, shock treatment has been applied in various parts of the world where it has usually meant macro-economic stabilization (particularly the control of hyper-inflation). It has had a different connotation in the case of post-communist economies which are characterized, in general, by extreme rigidity of resource movement, ignorance as to the functioning of organized markets and the lack of a proper institutional set-up, a supporting ethos and the necessary cultural base. In such circumstances policy should be targeted at the transformation of the societal body - which means institutional change, cultural change and material reconstruction. On this basis one can consider a theoretical underpinning of the policies of transformation beyond intuitions: there is a limit to tolerance of social sacrifice; time cannot be compressed at will. Development economists in particular have been unhappy with oversimplifications regarding the economics of transition.[29]

One way to proceed is to link theoretical explanations of the two competing visions within the paradigm provided by neo-classical analytics: equilibrium economics. One of them, best represented by classical macro-economics, rejects any state intervention in the economy since economic agents, it argues, optimize using all available information (in contrast, for example, with agents' 'bounded rationality' (Simon, 1958), thereby securing full price flexibility and hence fast and efficient allocation of resources. According to this view any rate of unemployment is 'natural' since it expresses agents' preferences. The other view starts from the assumption that prices are rigid to an extent sufficient to induce adjustments through quantity as well, so that aggregate demand equilibrates with aggregate supply below full employment: a non-Walrasian equilibrium. Both views are concerned with the functioning of a market economy. If the command system is viewed as a pathological form of the market economy, wherein structural dysfunctionalities are extreme, a hypothesis can be proposed: implementation of 'shock treatment' will add to a significant drop in production in the first phase. In this stage of the process of transformation entrenched structures have to be broken and changed, which means that the quantity of *friction*[30] inside the system goes up considerably and important energies (resources) are consumed in order to accommodate, adjust and change. Many characteristic features of this stage can be attributed to a change in the organizational behaviour of economic actors (Murrell, 1991). In this phase of the transition there is a dangerous territory over which both commands and markets - as regulatory mechanisms - do not function according to their logic, and to the congenital inefficiency of the old (to a large extent still existing) system is added the net inefficiency caused by friction.[31] This perspective is illuminated by interesting insights from 'structuralist macro-economics' (Taylor, 1991a, 1991b) which can highlight some of the perverse effects of 'orthodox' policies undertaken during transition.[32]

Within such a framework *hysteresis* phenomena can and should be tackled. Let us consider the increase in unemployment and the lasting effects of an open (unprotected) economy in a world dominated by imperfect markets. This is why shock therapy is met with reluctance by many people and why it demands much political courage and popular support to be applied. The sooner net costs turn into net benefits, the better for the political leadership - whose stock of political capital would, otherwise, be rapidly wiped out - not to mention for the population at large. One could argue that a gradualist policy cannot arrest the decline of output (living standards) as well. There is none the less a difference which explains why gradualist policies enjoy appeal with many political leaders and the population: when processes are under control a smaller, less brutal initial drop of output is likely compared to shock treatment. But when there is a collapse of the old institutional order and citizens rebel against any kind of authority,[33] and when, consequently, a 'free fall' syndrome is in full swing, gradualism itself presents pitfalls.

Another track of analysis would contrast the equilibrium approach with the evolutionary approach. Neo-classical economists pay less attention to social, behaviour-related and cultural aspects; for them the transformation of the system seems to be concerned, almost exclusively, with institutional rearrangements (reconstruction), the fundamental assumption being that economic agents are rational - they optimize - and would act accordingly should the environment be changed. It can be argued that the transformation under way in the former communist economies is a process with pronounced social and cultural dimensions. Involving the overcoming of inertia and ideological barriers, changing mentalities and psychologies[34] (the creation of a new social ethos appropriate for a market economy), a fierce struggle among 'coalitions of interests' (Olson, 1982), some of which support change whereas others wish to preserve the existing concentration of political and economic power. The clash of the various interests in society - during transition - raises the degree of autonomy of the process in the sense of reducing decision-makers' room to manoeuvre, should they want to force the pace of change.

A sociological (institutional) approach to the process of change tells us that in order to have a fair chance of progressing smoothly, the process needs to be backed by a strong coalition of interests - which means that a *social basis* in favour of change is necessary for it to occur; this 'reform constituency' cannot be built overnight. In the more backward post-communist societies this social constituency is still pretty feeble, which means that conservative forces are strong and can oppose change effectively. Seen in this way, transformation should not be conceived as a 'one-stroke policy'; since as a *real* process change cannot but be evolutionary, policy has to be shaped appropriately.

There is an additional factor that helps explain why shock treatments are harder to implement in laggard countries like Romania and the former Soviet republics; it is what I call a 'socially lived own experience', that compels people to think that 'there is no other way'. So long as a population - the largest, or the politically most vocal segments of it - tends to choose what it thinks involves the smallest immediate costs, a shock treatment is less likely to be undertaken or sustained for a long period of time (even if there is political goodwill); a muddling-through process is more likely. In this case the inconsistencies of the policy of transformation - and the resultant muddling-through of the process - can be related to the weakness of the social basis of change, which aggravates the very weaknesses of the policy itself, which are due to our limited knowledge.

An evolutionary (sociological) approach to understanding the dynamics of change and the likelihood of various policies to be applied would suggest a reconsideration of the partial reforms in Hungary and Poland. If one takes into account the process of 'learning' that these societies have been undergoing, including the acquisition of the aforementioned 'lived own experience' and the formation of a social basis, including an entrepreneurial class, for change, it is not hard to see the handicaps facing latecomers in the process.

The 'learning process' for society as a whole has to be linked with a 'limit rate of absorption of change'.This highlights a major paradox of Eastern European societies - especially the more backward among them - namely, their huge, practically limitless, thirst for information (novelty or change) coexisting with a limited capacity (both mental and infrastructural) to process this most important resource. A facet of this limitation is the problem identified by many experts - the region's limited capacity to absorb foreign capital productively - an issue different from that of using foreign assistance to create a 'safety net' during transition. When foreign assistance shifts upwards its 'learning curve' of a society's capacity for absorbing change is automatically increased. It is clear that the limit rate of absorption of change can put a further brake on the desire to speed up change.

Another major paradox affects the conditions which enhance a rapid transformation. The more ingredients of a market environment there are in a national space (the greater the comparative advantage of those who have started reform earlier) and the more favourable the political prerequisites are, the easier it is to transform quickly. On the other hand, the worse the state of the economy and the more wanting in terms of political and social prerequisites[35] is the national space, the more urgent and the more difficult it is to apply radical treatment. Urgency as an economically defined need cannot lead to wise measures if social and political factors are overlooked. It would seem that there is a time schedule according to which the 'jump into the unknown' follows a U-shaped curve so that there is a point of least-cumulated risk. This minimum-risk point is where the transformation policy is most likely to succeed. If it is assumed that, sooner or late, a radical treatment will be applied - for gradualism can only postpone some harsh measures - this point signals the moment to start shock therapy. This kind of reasoning may appear too speculative. Nevertheless, it hints at a paradoxical situation and at various trade-offs decision-makers have to make in order to identify the best route. Decision-makers overshoot or undershoot as markets do - which means that they can rush things above the 'natural rate of adjustment'[36] of society, or underestimate the potential for change of the social body. Since policy over- or undershooting is practically unavoidable, an important policy aim should be to reduce and respond to deviation as much and as quickly as possible. Another interesting question is on which side policy error is to be preferred, assuming that the goal of keeping the deviation at a minimum is kept in sight. Here one deals with both objective and subjective elements in making a judgement.

The optimization implied above, which sounds neo-classical, could be attacked on the grounds that the very actions of policy-makers generate and assimilate new information and, more significantly, change the environment.[37] In other words, the difference is between discovering the best route before starting the journey, or finding it along the way - 'creating it'. I believe that the two approaches can be reconciled by bearing in mind that corrections *sur le terrain* are easier to make the more knowledgeable and the better equipped the travellers are.

There is another factor that is common to policies derived from the different approaches: the time pressure exerted by the disintegration of old institutional structures, by the previously mentioned 'rebellion of citizens' (who defy any authority). This pressure induces the new power-holders, who have to cope with the syndrome of 'free fall' in economic activity, to resort to the presumed effectiveness of the disciplining power of impersonal market forces.

In my opinion, irrespective of the circumstances and the dominant vision espoused by policy-makers, several contending priorities have to be considered. First, the creation of an institutional and legal set-up fitting a market environment, including the formation of a safety-net, which is indispensable if we think that people are accustomed to view job security and low and stable prices for basic consumer goods as 'public goods' provided by the state. Second, privatization, and on a large scale, particularly at grass-roots level takes much time, has to be encouraged by all means available for both economic and social reasons: economically, since it leads to higher efficiency (even if domestic prices are still wrong and allocative efficiency does not improve dramatically); and socially, because it nurtures the entrepreneurial class as the main component of the social constituency favouring the transformation of the system. Third, price reform should be closely linked with income control within a policy-mix framework that proceeds from the major features of the environment; a system of industrial relations should be built upon the reality of the role workers play as both labour suppliers and potential enterprise owners or 'manager-monitors'. Finally, an industrial policy should be devised in keeping with the need to maintain a balance between market-induced destruction and construction; this policy should enhance the positive effects of the operation of market forces.

The magnitude of intended change, the prodigious uncertainties and the lack of sufficient knowledge on how to respond to the myriad of unforeseen developments are shaping transformation as a muddling-through process relying on trial and error procedures and showing a pattern of stop-go policies, including reversals.[38] Front-runner countries will have a less difficult time in maintaining the overall course of policy within a 'winning' corridor, whereas laggard countries will experience larger zigzags. But much will also depend on the quality of governance - the political and administrative elites.

I would also point out several fallacies which characterize the thinking of many laymen and even some fellow economists. One should not assume that a relatively well-functioning market economy, *ipso facto*, would secure the prosperity enjoyed by Western nations; Western prosperity relies on a high development level of productive apparatus and a degree of homogeneity of the factors of production. Second, it would be a mistake to presume that transformation will necessarily turn Eastern European economies into relatively well-functioning economies; the outcome for the foreseeable future is likely to be comparatively weak and less competitive (*quasi*) market economies. Third, past policy mistakes have to be considered, for they are a legacy to cope with; they can have a lasting impact and shape the course of events to come.

4. A further look ahead

What also makes the post-communist transition difficult is the legacy of pervasive moral crisis. It is hard to build new institutions when truth-telling, trust and loyalty are scarce commodities. As Arrow said: 'They are goods ... they have real, practical, economic value; they increase the efficiency of the system, enable you to produce more goods or more of whatever value you hold in high esteem' (1974, p. 23). The events since 1989 could not overcome this legacy, and the scarcity of such public goods has enhanced friction in society against the background of citizens' rebellion - its concrete forms being violence, all kinds of crime, 'rent-seeking' and free-riding as increasingly widespread behaviour. Two major lessons can be drawn in this respect. First, that the production of intangible goods - the moral reconstruction of society - is essential to the recovery of the output of material goods and services; the former 'crowds in' the latter. Second, trust, truth-telling and loyalty can substitute for tangible goods to a significant degree - particularly important when recession is a dangerously long-lasting event.

By admitting the hypothesis of the fundamental operational importance of intangibles, the political and *moral* dimension of the process of transformation comes to the fore. Credibility and trust need carriers, and these can only be individuals of high moral and political standards, who can provide effective leadership and rally support behind the goals of transformation. When the moral legitimacy of new power-holders is questionable, as occurred in Romania after Ceausescu's downfall, real institutional change is easily blocked.

The historical circumstances of Central and Eastern Europe make it hard, almost impossible, to dissociate political change from economic change.[39] Romania's experience shows how entrenched vested interests connected with the old regime have slowed down or rendered reforms insubstantial, or have promoted wrong policies. For example, the first (provisional) government adopted populist measures before the May elections of 1990; these measures helped the Salvation Front[40] win the elections, but worsened the state of the economy and compounded a stunning discrepancy between the electoral platform of the Front and the 'New Economic Policy' ushered in by Prime Minister Petre Roman and his 'young Turks' after the tragic events of June 1990 (culminating with the miners' rampage in Bucharest).[41]

There is a growing feeling in all the countries in the region that a complete 'hands-off' reform policy on the part of the governments cannot be justified not only because of the lack of institutional prerequisites for market forces to operate effectively, but also because the simple fact is that these forces, alone, would impose unbearable costs on the social body. In Central and Eastern Europe we deal with markets in their infancy; they need to be nurtured and even protected in a world of imperfect information and competition. There is need and scope for an industrial policy which aims at helping restructuring to respond to market signals, and at protecting the main asset of these societies - segments of highly skilled labour and a large pool of scientific and technical intelligentsia. A paradox of these societies is that striking ignorance coexists with tremendous intellectual and labour capabilities; this combination obscures the potential for progress by an apparent across-the-board depreciation of the factors of production. Capital and technology inflows as well as the functional opening of the economies would counteract this depreciation but they could impose undue hardships on the economy; hence the need for an imaginative industrial policy.

Industrial policy is also critical in bridging the gap between the effectiveness of controlling demand and that of stimulating supply. Supply responsiveness is so low that stabilizations are hardly sustainable. By industrial policy I mean a mix that connects income-control measures to industrial restructuring undertaken by public authorities which are responding to information provided by emerging markets. The goals would be to put a lid on inflation, alleviate unemployment (to cope with the hysteresis phenomena) and promote exports. Such a policy is all the more urgently needed when the 'social pie' is so small, redistribution effects are impacting negatively on many people and effective safety-nets are not in place. A scheme I favour strongly links incomes with the dynamics of saleable output, as proposed by Weitzman, (1984). Thus, assuming that market-clearing prices operate (and that optimal sizes for producing units are observable, or can be estimated) enterprises can be split into three categories: negative valued-added units, unprofitable (but still positive valued-added producing) units and profitable enterprises. Negative value-added enterprises should be closed down without delay; it is less costly to pay workers unemployment benefits and retrain them than to keep these enterprises running. Profitable units do not present any problem since they are good businesses. The zone of concern for policy-makers is represented by unprofitable enterprises which under normal conditions (with sufficient flexibility of resources) would have to be done away with. The idea is to resort to a phased elimination according to a timetable that is founded on the minimization of costs of adjustment. There are key variables in the scheme: unemployment benefit and an additional income provided by the state to workers so that they have an incentive to continue working instead of taking unemployment benefit.

Unprofitable enterprises would be targeted for a gradual phasing-out so that unemployment be attenuated and its cost redistributed over time. At the same time, public authorities would have an easier task in securing resources for a safety-net and for facilitating labour reallocation through training programmes. The crux of the matter lies in convincing workers of the benefits of this scheme for the economy as a whole and for each of the targeted enterprises. This could be achieved as part of a social compact within the framework of an industrial relations agreement that sees workers as an active voice in the management of transformation. It could be argued that this scheme may slow down restructuring: that is a valid argument, but only if social and political constraints are dismissed. For the sake of process sustainability there are many reasons for advocating an industrial policy.

In Romania (as in the former Soviet Union) another critical issue is the turning around of agriculture. Yields are very low, which means that there is much room for improvement. People devote more than 60 per cent of their incomes to the procuring of essentials, so a major boost in agricultural output - with a corresponding drop in the relative prices of food - would raise living standards dramatically and help transformation. The major stumbling block is that land reform, by itself, creates friction while new property rights are being established and, additionally, price liberalization produces a shock to the urban population by turning the terms of trade against it.[42] But the stakes are too high to turn away from focusing attention on a sector which is most likely to lead the recovery of the economy.

Were I asked about Romania's long-term prospects I would answer that its economy is like an underrated stock in a world stock exchange. Warren Buffett's philosophy about investments - that one should think in terms of fundamentals - is very much in my way of thinking. But I also remember a discussion I had with Thomas Gibbons, an American diplomat who, listening to me and agreeing with my view, made the meaningful remark: 'In this region *all* countries are like underrated stocks'. The implication is that the governance issue is of paramount importance for long-term dynamics. And since the quality of governance seen as a common denominator of succeeding government teams and of the structures underneath them is a huge variable in the equation of transformation, predictions about long-term prospects are a more than normally risky business. What is, nevertheless, certain is that those countries which can practise good, healthy politics will find it much easier to practise good, successful economics.

A final word is reserved for the involvement of the developed West in the process. In the last few years academics and the media in the USA have been debating the causes of the relative decline of the American economy; much ink has been expended expounding on the stakeholder vs. shareholder issue in order to throw light on what secures highly performing governance at the corporate level. One can make an analogy and view the ex-communist countries as bankrupt entities which need to be restructured and turned into efficient economic systems. Since the West is vitally interested in the recovery of these entities, it has to act like a *stakeholder* - with a deep moral, political and economic commitment - and not like a simple shareholder. Such an attitude will help considerably to solve the governance issue (both at macro- and micro-economic levels) in Central and Eastern Europe and make the transition easier.

Further Reading

Akerlof, G., Yelen, J. (eds), (1987), *Efficiency Wage Models of the Labor Market*. Cambridge, Cambridge University Press.

Arrow, J.K. (1974), *The Limits of Organization*. New York, Norton.

Axenciuc, V. (1971) 'The Romanian Economy in the First Half of the Twentieth Century' (in Romanian), in: Postolache. T. (ed.), *Romanian Economy in the Twentieth Century* (in Romanian), Bucharest, Editura Academiei, pp. 99-173.

Barro, R., Grossman, H. (1974) 'Suppressed Inflation and the Supply Multiplier'.*Review of Economic Studies*, Vol. 41, 1, pp. 87-104.

Ben-ner, A., Montias, J.M. (1991) 'The Introduction of Markets in a Hypercentralized Economy - the case of Romania'. *Journal of Economic Perspectives*, Vol. 5, 4, pp. 163-170.

Bhagwati, J. (1958) 'Immiserising Growth - a geometrical note. *Review of Economic Studies*, 25. Also (1968) 'Distortions and Immiserising Growth - a generalization'.*Review of Economic Studies*, 35.

Brada, J., King, A. (1986), 'Taut Plans, Repressed Inflation and the Supply of Effort in Centrally Planned Economies'. *Economics of Planning*, Vol. 20, 3, pp. 162-178.

Calvo, G., Coricelli, F. (1992), 'Stagflationary Effects of Stabilization Programs in Reforming Socialist Countries: Enterprise-Side and Household-Side Factors'. *World Bank Review*, Vol. 6, 1, pp. 71-90.

Chirot, D. (ed.), (1989), *The Origins of Backwardness in Eastern Europe*. Berkeley, University of California Press.

Csaba, L. (1991), 'First Lessons of Transforming the Economic System in Central Europe'. Budapest, July, manuscript.

Daianu, D. (1984), 'External Equilibrium and the Type of Control of Domestic Absorption'. *Revue Roumaine de Sciences Sociales-série économique*, 2, pp. 115-136.

Daianu, D. (1987) 'On Aggregate (Dis)equilibrium and Performance: Supply-vs. Demand-Constrained Economies'. *Revue Roumain de Sciences Sociales-série économique*, 1, pp. 31-65.

Etzioni, A.(1991), 'A Socio-economic Perspective on Friction'. Study.prepared for the IAREP/SASE Conference, manuscript.

Gelb, A., Gray, C. (1991), *The Transformation of Economies in Central and Eastern Europe*. Washington DC., The World Bank.

Hankiss, E. (1988), 'The 'Second Society': Is there an Alternative Social Model Emerging in Hungary'. Washington DC., Woodrow Wilson Center, occasional paper 16.

Hirsch, S. (1977), 'Rich Man's. Poor Man's and Every Man's Goods. Aspects of Industrialization'. Tübingen, J.C.B. Mohr (Paul Siebeck), *Kieler Studien*, 148.

Holzman, Fr. (1979), 'Some Theories of the Hard Currency Shortages of Centrally Planned Economies' in: *Soviet Economy in a Time of Change* - a compendium of papers submitted to the JOC, US Congress, Washington DC., USGPO, pp. 297-316.

Johnson, H. (1967), 'The Possibility of Income Losses from increased Efficiency of Factor Accumulation in the Presence of Tariffs'. *Economic Journal*.

Klaus, V., Ježek, T. (1989), 'The Evolutionary Aproach'. *Financial Times*, December 13, p. 15.

Kochanowitz, J. (1991), 'Is Poland Unfit for Capitalism? Poland in the 1980s and the 1990s : Social Change in Historical Perspective'. Paper prepared for a Conference on 'Dilemmas of Transition in East Central Europe', Center for European Studies, Harvard University, March 15-17, manuscript.

Koopmans, Th., Montias, J.M. (1972), 'On the Description and Comparison of Economic Systems' in: Ecktein (ed.), *Comparison of Economic Systems. Theoretical and Methodological Approaches*. Berkeley, University of California Press.

Lallement, J. (1991), 'Corporatisme Societal et Emploi'.'*CFDT Aujourd'hui*, September.

Leijonhufvud, A. (1968), *On Keynesian Economics and the Economics of Keynes*. London, Oxford Univeristy Press.

Linden, R. (1989), 'Romania: The Search for Economic Sovereignty' in: *Pressure for Reform in Eastern European Economies*. Vol, 12, JEC, October 27.

Manoilescu, M. (1934), *Théorie du Protectionnisme et de l'Échange International*. Paris. Also (1934), *Le Siẑcle du Corporatisme*. Paris.

Montias, J.M. (1991), 'The Romanian Economy: a Survey of Current Economic Problems.' *European Economy*, Special edition, June, pp. 177-198.

Murrell, P. (1991, a), 'Evolution in Economics and in the Economic Reform of the Centrally Planned Economies'. Manuscript.

Murrell, P. (1991, b), 'Can Neoclassical Economics Underpin the Reform of Centrally Planned Economies?' *Journal of Economic Perspectives*, Vol. 5,

4, pp. 59-76.

Myint, H. (1971), *Economic Theory and Underdeveloped Countries*. New York.

Nelson, R., Winter, S. (1982), *An Evolutionary Theory of Economic Change*. Cambridge, Mass. Harvard University Press.

North, D. (1981), *Structure and Change in Economic History*. New York, Norton.

Ofer, G. (1990), 'Decelerating Growth under Socialism: The Soviet Case'. February, first draft manuscript.

Olson, M. (1982), *The Rise and Decline of Nations, Economic Growth, Stagflation and Social Rigidities*. New Haven, Yale University Press.

Olson, M., Murrell, P. (1991), 'The Devolution of Centrally Planned Economies'. January, manuscript.

Perkins, D. (1991), 'Developing Nations Now Turn to the Market Economy Concept'. A conversation in *The Harvard Gazette*. July 26.

Rönnas, P. (1990), 'The Economic Legacy of Ceausescu'. Stockholm Institute of Soviet and East European Economics. Working paper, no. 11.

Schmitter, Ph. (1974), 'Still The Century of Corporatism?' *Review of Politics*, January, pp. 85-131.

Shafir, M. (1985), *Romania: Politics, Economics and Society*. London, F. Pinter.

Simon, H. (1959), 'Theories of Decision-Making in Economics and Behavioural Sciences'. *American Economic Review*, Vol. 49, 3, pp. 253-283.

Smith, A. (1990), 'The Romanian Economy: Policy and Prospects for the 1990s'. Paper prepared for a NATO colloquium, Brussels, April.

Taylor, L. (1983), *Structuralist Macroeconmics*. New York, Basic Books.

Taylor, L. (1988), *Varieties of Stabilization Experience*. Oxford, Clarendon Press.

Taylor, L. (1991, a), 'The Post-Socialist Transition from a Development Economics Point of View'. MIT, August, manuscript.

Taylor, L.(1991b), *Income Distribution, Inflation and Growth*. Cambridge MA, MIT.

Teodorescu, A. (1991), 'The Romanian Economy: The Future of a Failure' in: Sjobery, O., Wyzan, M. (eds.) *Economic Change in the Balkan States*. St Martin's Press, New York.

Tismaneanu, V. (1990), 'Understanding National Stalinism: A Comparative Approach to the History of Romanian Communism'. Washington DC, Woodrow Wilson Center, occasional paper, no. 25.

Weitzman, M. (1984), *The Share Economy*. Cambridge, Harvard University Press.

Winiecki, J. (1991), 'The Inevitability of a Fall in Output in the Early Stages of Transition to the Market: Theoretical Underpinnings'. *Soviet Studies*, no. 4, pp. 669-676.

Wood, A. (1990), 'A Nominal Pause, But Some Real Progress'. *Financial Times*, October 4, p. 19.

Notes

1   J. Kornai is, I believe, the first who argued in favour of using the notion of 'transformation' as against 'reform', in order to convey the magnitude and complexity of the process.

2   It is noteworthy that Nobel prize-winners, apart from rare interviews, do not seem to be engaged in this intellectual endeavour, a fact which is quite puzzling.

3   The undisputed theoretical 'guru' was M. Manoilescu (1929-34) who advocated industrial protectionism and corporatism. Interestingly enough, after Ph. Schmitter (1974) drew attention to Manoilescu's seemingly lasting ideas about social development in this century, some are construing 'neo-corporatism' as a way out of the malaise of industrial societies and, implicitly, as a venue for institutional reconstruction in Central and Eastern Europe. Lallement (1991).

4   A survey of the interwar evolution of the Romanian economy was recently made available by Axenciuc (1991).

5   According to Solimano in 1937, nominal income per capita was estimated at $440 in Great Britain and $400, $340, $330, $306, $265 and $190 in Sweden, Germany, Belgium, Netherlands, France and Austria respectively. The corresponding estimates for Czechoslovakia, Hungary, Poland, Romania, Yugoslavia and Bulgaria were $170, $120, $100, $81, $80 and $75 respectively (Gelb A. & Gray C. (1991), p. 65). See also Ben-ner and Montias (1991), p. 163

6   It can be likened to Leijonhufvud's, (1968) corridor within which '... the system's homeostatic mechanisms work well ...'. p. 32.

7   Remark made during the Romanian-American economic roundtable held in Bucharest, 16-17 April 1991.

8   By creating 'big industry' communism produced an oversized working class which, ironically, helped bring about its collapse. But workers can slow down or derail 'transformation' because of entrenched vested interests. See also Kochanowicz (1990) on the preparedness of workers to accept capitalism.

9   Thus, 'Russia is no longer the undifferentiated peasant country it was when Stalin embarked on his crash-course communism. In 1939 only thirty-two per cent of the Russian population lived in towns and cities...Now it is seventy-four per cent...It has ninety-nine per cent literacy rate, ninety-six per cent enrolment in secondary education, and a large educated scientific and managerial elite'. (*The Economist*, 7 December 1991, p. 28).

10   The role of religion in the West, as compared to the East, can be mentioned here.

11 The German and the Japanese models can be juxtaposed to the Anglo-Saxon model; the former two evince a higher degree of co-operation among government, business leaders and trade unions and also a sense of solidarity (communitarian values) that might be very attractive to many Central and Eastern Europeans.

12 Romanian communist leaders can be viewed as having been very nationalistic since they steadfastly opposed Moscow's wishes for close economic integration. But I submit that the clever nationalists were those who succeeded in distancing their economies from the traditional (Stalinist) model of functioning. In this vein, Hungarians, Poles and others can be considered as not having been less nationalistic; on the contrary. Thus nationalism in policy takes on a more subtle meaning which goes beyond the simple acts of defying the Superpower and relates to an understanding of the overall functioning of society. This is what made possible in Hungary the existence and development of a 'second economy' and a 'second society' (Hankiss 1988). In this respect I remember an article in the Italian communist weekly *Rinascita*, in the late 1980s, which decried the intellectual paucity of those commanding the heights of the Romanian Communist Party (not only the two Ceausescus). I wonder what would have been the evolution of the quality of the Party apparatus should L. Patrascanu (an outstanding intellectual and a leader of the Party who was purged and subsequently murdered in the early 1950s) and not Gh. Gheorghiu Dej (Ceausescu's predecessor and the one responsible for Patrascanu's death) have been at its helm. One can think in terms of both doctrine and policy. I assume that Patrascanu - should he have been able to stay in power, which is questionable for various reasons - would not have allowed Ceausescu-like-minded people to surround him (for a brief but excellent analysis of 'National Stalinism' see Tismaneanu 1990).

13 For a good coverage of the whole period see, for instance, Linden (1989), Montias (1991), Rönnas (1990), Smith, (1990), Teodorescu (1990).

14 By institutional arrangements I understand also 'the rules of the game' enjoying wide social acceptability; it is a broad sense which can be found in the works of North (1981).

15 Koopmans and Montias used this function in a seminal paper (1972). I also used it in order to deal with the 'performance deficit' of supply constrained economies (Daianu 1984, 1987).

16 By the end of the 1960s Ceausescu was getting a firm grip on the leadership of the Party and felt no more need for 'renewal' gestures. Moreover, the events in Czechoslovakia in 1968 convinced him that relaxation of control endangered his supremacy by loosening reform forces within society and by tainting his image as a staunch upholder of ideological 'purity' (which was a bargaining chip in his conflict with Moscow).

17 As Shafir nicely put it, it was an example of 'simulated change' (1985).

18 Market relations operate in any kind of environment; I have in mind officially sanctioned market transactions and corresponding institutions like those encouraged by partial reforms in Hungary and Poland.

19 The average annual share of accumulation (in current prices) in the net material product was stated to be 25.5 per cent for 1961-65; 29.5 per cent for 1966-70; 33.7 per cent for 1971-75; and 35.3 per cent for 1976-80. (1986), *Statistical Yearbook*. Bucharest, p. 60.

20 The share of CMEA countries in the overall trade went from just over 80 per cent in the 1950s to 34.6 per cent in 1980 (CMEA data).

21 Command economies are cybernetic systems based on chain links, as compared to market economies that use, prevailingly, parallel connections. With growing complexity the recoverability of command economies gets much lower than that of market-based systems.

22 What Ofer aptly calls 'haste' (1990).

23 See Bhagwati (1958, 1968) and Johnson (1967), especially.

24 Holzman talked about 'the saleability illusion' in this respect (1979).

25 Barro and Grossman (1974); for a command economy see Brada and King (1986).

26 Hirsch has called it a 'sequence of industrialization' (1977).

27 Imports of machinery and equipment from the developed market economies were one third in the late 1980s as compared to the level at the beginning of the decade.

28 Efficiency-wage models (Akerlof and Yelen 1987) could be used to explain the impact of the decline of living standards on labour supply, particularly when the drop is extreme.

29 For instance D. Perkins, the Director of the Harvard Institute of International Development, expresses his misgivings about the big-bang approach (1991, p. 6-7).

30 Etzioni (1991) has an interesting elaboration on *friction* during transition.

31 Winiecki considers that much of the loss of output is benefactory, not to be seen as additional inefficiency (1991).

32 Analysing 'stagflationary effects of stabilization policies' in reforming economies, Calvo and Coricelli (1992) emphasize the similarities between the 'enterprise-side view' and the neo-structuralist approach.

33 This happened in Romania after December 1989.

34 Murrell (1991 a, b) is a leading advocate of an evolutionary approach to the economics of transition. For the general framework of this approach see Nelson and Winter (1982). Among the Eastern European economists, Csaba, who is a refined analyst and a well-known observer of the whole region, has similar views (1991).

35 The feasibility (sustainability) of shock treatment depends on a series of critical social, political and cultural components of the fabric of society.

For such a treatment to be initiated, the goodwill of the political leadership needs to meet the goodwill of the population (the latter involving the existence of charismatic and trustworthy leaders, who can shape the public mood and energize individual and collective actions). This occurred in Poland, which still looks like an exceptional case. The therapy applied in Hungary is clearly of a milder sort, and the same can be said of what was attempted in the Federal Czech and Slovak Republic. I stress this because however determined a governmental team is to start radical change, its ultimate decision will be a function of the responsiveness of the population. A policy that does not meet such requirements - running also counter to the preparedness of people to accept sacrifices - will inexorably become bogged down and emasculated.

36 The 'natural rate of adjustment' of society can be defined as an imagined optimal speed of change that maximizes society's preference (welfare) function.

37 In a programmatic article in *The Financial Times*, Klaus and Ježek approvingly cite Brzeski: 'just as the optimal allocation of resources cannot be achieved outside the market process, because the process itself generates the necessary information, so in the overhaul of an entire system, only the actual steps taken can disclose the acceptable path' (1989, p. 15).

38 A distinction has to be made between reform as a *real process* and reform as *policy*; the real process can move forward even when reform as a policy might experience setbacks. This is the point made by Wood when distinguishing between 'nominal pause' and 'real progress' (1990, p. 19).

39 As compared to China, where reforms initiated from above have been tightly maintained within an economic tunnel.

40 The political formation which appeared after the overnight collapse of the Communist Party.

41 'The New Economic Policy' highlighted an increasing influence of the liberal (in the European sense) wing within the ruling strata of the Salvation Front together with the desire to gain credibility abroad after the unfortunate events of June of that year. This policy would get a new radical twist in September 1990 as the economy was getting even more out of control.

42 Actually the shock is smaller if it is considered that a large part of the urban population is closely linked with the countryside, that many city dwellers stand with one leg in a village where they might own a house and a plot. The inference is that a substantial amount of what goes out of one pocket goes into the other pocket. None the less, there are people - like retired persons, some of those with fixed incomes - who are badly hurt by price liberalization should they not be able to enter, or re-enter the labour market by converting their additional available time (previously used as search and queuing time) into an attractive labour supply.

CHAPTER SEVEN

After the Collapse of East Germany: Social Insecurity and Political Disillusion in the New *Länder*

Jörg Roesler

1. The 'Big Bang' introduction of market economy in East Germany

There can be no doubt that the East German economy in the 1980s lagged remarkably behind that of the Federal Republic of Germany. Estimates of the gross domestic product undertaken during the second half of the 1980s from different Western economic institutions showed a gap of between 46 per cent and 52 per cent.[1] Nevertheless it was a functioning economy with GDP growth rates in the second half of the 1980s between 2 per cent and 4 per cent.[2] The GDR had the highest productivity standard within the CMEA.[3]

During the revolution in autumn 1989 up to summer 1990 growth ceased, the output began to drop, but modestly. In the first half of 1990 production in manufacturing industries had fallen to 93 per cent, compared with 1989 (=100 per cent). This relatively favourable economic development was due to three factors: the revolution proceeded peacefully, the Modrow coalition government (November 1989 to April 1990) was relatively successful in creating stability and the following de Maiziere government, mainly engaged in bargaining with the government of the Federal Republic about the proposed currency union, did not make many institutional changes until 1 July 1990, the day of the currency union.[4]

The East and West German governments were convinced that the conversion of the East German currency into Deutschmarks would enable the East Germans to catch up with the productivity and consumption level of the Federal Republic within a short period.[5] Currency union meant economic integration at once. Through currency union the GDR also lost the most important instrument of a more gradual adaptation to Western markets - the exchange rate mechanism.

The economic consequences of currency union were unforeseen and formidable. The currency conversion affected the GDR economy like a revaluation of its currency by about 300-400 per cent. East German producers got into trouble on Western markets, where they had been able to compete before 1990 only by taking into account financial losses, refunded by the state. But the main problems arose on the domestic market. The *de facto* revaluation of the GDR-Mark meant that goods from Western Germany could push out GDR products. Other reasons were the lower quality of the goods in the East, and the better design, especially of consumer products, of goods in the West; also East German consumer goods were increasingly excluded from the supermarkets when West German trade chains gained control over these.[6] This led to a sharp decline of industrial production, the backbone of the GDR economy. In the first month after currency union production in industry dropped disastrously. In July 1990 it fell to 55.4 per cent of the 1989 level.[7] In the beginning the East European export markets remained untouched. Many enterprises tried even to raise exports in order to compensate for the losses on the domestic market, but with limited success. Industrial production remained at 51 per cent of the 1989 level during the second half of 1990. But this did not mean stabilization at a lower level. Beginning with 1991 the former East bloc countries should have had to pay hard currency for their imports from the former GDR. But they simply could not afford it. They cancelled most of the export orders to East German enterprises. This led to a further fall of industrial production in the former GDR during the first half of 1990 to a level of 33 per cent, compared with 1989.[8]

Much hope for investments of West German enterprises in the East was connected with privatization. This was organized by the *Treuhandanstalt*, a holding company which had taken over all former state-owned property. Privatization really began in autumn 1990 and accelerated in 1991. Never-the-less private investments in industry fell far below expectations. On the other hand the enterprises, remaining in *Treuhand*, became subject to 'passive restructuring', i.e. they had to give up large parts of the production programme and workforce without getting investments for real modernization.[9] While opinions about the economic efficiency of the privatization concept of *Treuhand* differ,[10] there is no doubt that a certain property regulation in the unity treaty, which came into effect in October 1990, did utmost harm to the recovery of the crisis-ridden East German economy: paragraph 41 gave former owners of property of all kinds the right to demand its return.[11] Since then the 'Offices for Unresolved Ownership Questions' have not been able to catch up with the flood of applications for the return of property. In spring 1995 there were about 2.4 million applications demanding the return of property items. Of these 90 per cent concern the return of real estate. Therefore in many cases, especially in inner-city regions, investments have been hampered.[12] The level of production in manufacturing industry also remained low in 1992 (35 per cent of the 1989 level).[13] Beginning with 1993 industrial production increased. After a peak of 20 per cent growth in 1994 the speed of catching up on the West slowed down to 8 per cent in 1995, to 5 per cent in 1996, and, according to prognosis, to 4 per cent in 1997. Only some industrial branches have reached the 1989 production level, on the average 50 per cent of the volume of the last year of the planned economy has reached.[14]

2. Unemployment: the main source of social insecurity

When in November 1989 the Modrow government came into power, it did not pay much attention to unemployment.[15] Partly this was due to the lack of any experience with overt unemployment in East Germany for decades. The last reported figures for unemployment in East Germany for decades. The last reported figures for unemployment in the GDR before 1990 date back to 1958, when the number was 11,000, compared with 66,000 at the beginning of 1955 and 325,000 in 1950, the year after the foundation of the East German state. Between 1955 and 1959 government spending on unemployment decreased from 9.5 to 2.2 million Marks, e.g. not more than 2.3 per cent of all labour-related state expenditure.[16]

But during the first quarter of 1990 it became obvious that a certain amount of temporary unemployment would be unavoidable. In February, three important laws were passed concerning the unemployed: the state and enterprises had to share the costs; the state took over the costs of retraining. And the labour exchange (*Arbeitsamt*) was adapted to the new conditions in March 1990.[17]

One month after the elections in March 1990 the de Maiziere government came into power. In his first speech as Prime Minister, de Maiziere underlined state support for those who would become unemployed as a result of rationalization and closures of environmentally dangerous and outdated factories. He expected - as Modrow did - unemployment to be temporary and was convinced private enterprises would soon flourish. De Maiziere was confident that the losses in working places would be compensated by 500,000 new jobs, to be created by the expected upswing of the East-German economy after the disappearance of the bottlenecks of the planned economy by currency union.[18]

For Prime Minister de Maiziere an extension of the employment legislation, introduced by his predecessor, seemed to be unnecessary for two reasons: the measure undertaken by Modrow was sufficient to cope with the expected frictional and temporary increase of unemployment. He also knew that with the day of currency union the whole framework of economic and social legislation was to be changed according to West German patterns in any case. East Germany would benefit from an employment legislation which was assumed to be one of the most generous in the world.[19]

Only two months after this declaration, in July 1990, the de Maiziere government was faced with the problem of soaring unemployment. Enterprises, hit by the shrinking markets for their goods, tried to cut costs by dismissing large parts of their workforce. De Maiziere called Chancellor Kohl for help. The federal government had *de facto* to take over government responsibility from de Maiziere and to develop a labour market policy (LMP) for the east of Germany. Because the expected jump-started boom after the introduction of the market economy had failed, Bonn anticipated in summer 1990 an intensive but short adaptation crisis. For the proposed severe but temporary unemployment it hesitated to implement those measures of active labour market policy (ALMP) which it had tried to introduce in West Germany after having taken over the government from the social democrats in 1982, such as job creation (ABM = *Arbeitsbeschaffungsmaßnamen*), job training and short-time work (STW). But from the political point of view no time had to be lost. The election on the *Länder* level in East Germany had been fixed for September and the election for the Federal Diet was to take place in December. To hold on to power the Kohl government depended on an overwhelming victory in the East. Kohl and de Maiziere had promised that nobody's standard of living in East Germany should decline as a result of currency union. Many should soon enjoy a higher standard of living. This promise and the trust in the Christian Democrats (CDU) was at stake when the 'market adaptation crisis' arose during July and August. The Bonn administration's decision was not to interfere in the East German economy, which should further be rebuilt by market forces, but to fill the gap between the economic performance and the standard of living aspirations of the East German voters by massive payments to avoid registered unemployment from rocketing. Therefore, in relation to the decrease in production, only a small part of the workforce was laid off. The number of unemployed rose from 142,000 to 272,000 in July, to 361,000 in August and 445,000 in September. The official quota of registered unemployed did not surpass 5 per cent. Many more workers were transferred from full-time to short-time work (656,000 in July, 844,000 in August and 229,000 in September). Involuntary STW, up to that time unknown in the GDR, was used to cut production costs in 6000 enterprises in August and 20,000 in September.[20] Special regulations for state payments and additional financial help by *Treuhand* made it possible that short-time workers often earned 90 per cent of their former net income.[21] This solution seemed to be acceptable to all sides: the CDU-led government secured the trust of its voters in the East. The enterprises got rid of most of the costs of the unused workforce. It also seemed to make sense from the macro-economic point of view: the extension of short-time work was accompanied by the inauguration of a comprehensive job-training programme, paid for by the federal government and supported by West German trade unions and employer organizations. The aim was to retrain the unemployed and short-time workers according to West German industrial standards and professional structure.[22]

Acceptance of the newly introduced ALMP measures by the East German workforce differed. Endangered by unemployment, they preferred STW not only for financial reasons. The short-time worker could pretend to belong to the enterprise and hope to begin full-time work at the moment when the economic situation of the enterprise would allow it again. The social links between the workers and the factory and between groups of workers were not severed by STW. Short-time work was also simply accepted because overt unemployment was feared most. Losing one's job was perceived by the individual as a sign of personal failure. This belief partly resulted from the old GDR experience that everybody had a job or could get one. At that time those out of work, even temporarily, were thought to be more or less anti-social. Furthermore, the 'imported' popular Western ideology had led them to believe that anyone who really wished to work would find a job in a market economy and only lazy or incompetent people would remain unemployed.[23]

Job training as the other broadly offered ALMP was accepted much more hesitantly than STW by the East German employees. In the 'socialist' past, training was undertaken by workers to adapt them to new tasks within the framework of their existing workplaces. In 1990 retraining for an anonymous labour market was unknown and not expected.[24] Being trained for an unknown market seemed not to make sense. This thinking was underlined by the growing awareness that virtually every branch of the East German economy and every profession was hit by the crisis. The most appreciated retraining for 'secure' jobs seemed to be impossible. First experiences with the hastily created job centres also proved that many of the (mostly West German) private entrepreneurs were much more interested in obtaining a share of the billion Deutschmarks of government subsidies for retraining schemes than providing the workforce with adequate knowledge to be competitive in a market economy.[25] In 1990 and also 1991 the retraining courses offered exceeded demand.

Job creation was very rare in the beginning of mass unemployment in East Germany. The CDU-led Kohl government as well as the employers' associations disliked this way of reducing unemployment by ALMP more than other measures. But in February 1991 it became obvious that the often announced boom in the East German economy was not only delayed by some months as supposed by the federal government until late summer 1990, but would probably not come into being before the end of 1991. A Cologne-based economic institute forecast that unemployment would rise by one million if additional ALMP measures were not introduced.[26] Thus at least for the moment even the traditional opponents of ALMP in West German society remained silent when a new ALMP package was introduced for East-Germany during the first half of 1991 under the slogan, 'building bridges to the future'. More than a quarter of a million jobs were to be created in this way during 1991.[27]

But East German workers hesitated to accept this generous offer. They had enjoyed life-long secure jobs. Now they were expected to be grateful for the chance to be engaged for only two years and then to be thrown on the market again. STW had been accepted much more readily because it was seen only as an interruption between two periods of lasting employment - that in the 'socialist' past and that in the 'capitalist' future, when the adaptation crisis would be over. Against the worker's suspicions towards ABM its supporters in government and trade unions argued that in West Germany, on average, one out of two ABM labourers was able to secure a permanent job. But East Germans had learned that such a deep economic crisis in the old *'Länder'* had never been experienced and remained suspicious. The ABM based new ALMP variant started slowly. The politicians complained that the money for ABM was there, but lay idle.

Despite these mental hurdles - and some organizational ones also - ABM became widely accepted by East Germans after some months as an alternative to STW and unemployment because of the lack of new jobs. The idea was to transfer large parts of the former work places of reduced or shut-down industrial plants to ABM by removing decayed installations and buildings and eliminating environmental damages. These tasks made sense in the minds of the workers endangered by dismissals. They did understand: taking part in these variants of ABM could help to attract new investment on the site of old plant. To rebuild the communication lines between villages and towns could also help to improve the image of locations in the eyes of potential investors. What counted most for the workers was that they remained together in ABM groups as in former times in their workshops. They could leave home every morning as usual and did not get as frustrated as their unemployed neighbours. Nevertheless, especially because of the temporary character of the ABM work, it was not accepted as a full alternative to a 'real' job.[28] At the end of 1991 every eighth employee affected by LMP got his place by job creation. The ABM figure (391,000) was higher than the number engaged in job training (334,000).[29]

But when it became common knowledge that the economic crisis in the East would last into 1992 and mass unemployment would become a part of the future of the new *Länder* even after economic recovery had taken place, the (West German) employer associations again raised the fear that ABM places would turn into permanent state-subsidized jobs.

They demanded that the government should create, instead of ABM measures, additional places for job training. The government gave way to their grievances. In 1992 the money for job creation became more or less frozen. First signs of the new development in ALMP appeared in January 1992, when the number of ABM jobs remained nearly unchanged (394,000 against 391,000 in December), while the number of people in job training increased from 334,000 to 425,000.[30] As a result of the change in labour market policy, initiated in 1992, the number of ABM jobs kept falling to 201,000 by summer 1996. The number of persons in job training also decreased, but exceeded this figure slightly, i.e. 225,000 persons. The number of all ALMP jobs was reduced from 1,985,000 to 1,014,000 in 1995. In 1996 the Federal Government announced a scheme to curb ALMP funding up to the year 2000 by 20 billion Marks. This measure is bound further to increase the trend of reduction which has prevailed since 1992.[31]

The number of overt unemployed, which had passed the half-million mark in October 1990, and exceeded one million for the first time in July 1991, had in January 1992, with 1.343 million (unemployment quota 17.0 per cent), reached a new peak. The average number of overt unemployed remained in the following years constantly above one million in spite of the renewal of economic growth in all sectors of the economy, with a slight tendency to increase in 1995. The rate of unemployment was around 15 per cent during these years. Between 1989 and 1994 job losses differed remarkably between the sectors of the economy: while the number of jobs in the service sector increased by 91 per cent, it fell in all other sectors, especially in agriculture (by 77 per cent) and industry (by 51 per cent). Until 1994, on average 36 per cent of all jobs disappeared in the East German economy. General employment figures present some differences between the *Länder*. Until July 1996 Sachsen-Anhalt was hit worse (the rate of unemployment reached 17.5 per cent). The lowest rate of unemployment (14.6 per cent) was in Saxony. These figures include only registered unemployed. At the time of writing these lines there is widespread fear that, with additional cuts in ALMP expenditure during the forthcoming years the percentage of overt unemployment would reach 25 to 30 per cent of the East German labour force.[32]

3.   Political disillusion: the development of a distinct political society

The politicians in Bonn had up to 1992 successfully prevented the economic disaster turning into a social one, as far as real income was concerned. Real disposable income of private households averaged 12 per cent more in 1991 than in 1990, when it was higher than the 1989 level. This permitted households to step up private consumption, despite the emerging propensity to save. Private consumption rose year by year - starting from a lower level - faster than in the West. In 1991 the consumption level in the East was 51.4 per cent of that in the West of Germany, 66.1 per cent in 1994, and 67.8 per cent two years later. Private consumption rose faster than productivity in the East German economy, which in 1991 reached 31.0 per cent and in 1994 53.0 per cent of the West German level. The gap was not closed in the following years. In 1996 wages in the industry of the new *Länder* reached 66 per cent of the level of the old *Länder* , but only 49 per cent of their productivity.[33] The financial transfers explain how real income and economic growth could develop at different speeds. The mounting gap had to be paid (mainly for LMP) by the federal state. Total financial transfers to state and local authorities in East Germany reached 130.5 million in 1991 and peaked to 180 million Marks in 1994. The amount of transfers corresponded to 51.9 per cent of East German GDP. Since 1995 transfers have been reduced and are expected to be reduced further in the coming years. There are demands for closing the gap between productivity and income levels in the new *Länder* . Two of the six leading German economic research institutes (Deutsches Institut für Wirtschaftsforschung [DIW] and Institut für Wirtschaftsforschung, Halle [IWH] demanded a 20 per cent cut in East German wages to make entrepreneurship in the new *Länder* more profitable.[34] No other former socialist country has experienced such an amount of financial aid. The Germans in the East should be grateful for the help, insist the Germans in the West. They often argue that the only source of East German anxiety is exaggerated demand for material goods without the readiness to work as hard as the West Germans to reach their standard of living.

Such reproaches forget that, according to Chancellor Kohl's and Prime Minister de Maiziere's promises, the immediate catching up with the West German level of standard of living would be possible, if the Deutschmark and a market economy on the West German pattern were introduced in the GDR without hesitation. Indeed, the catching up of income in East Germany was remarkable, also in real terms for those who did not lose their jobs, though it was far from reaching the promised 100 per cent of West German level. Even for the year 2010 the DIW experts do not expect that East German wages will be in line with West German ones. The differences in the wage gap between

West and East of the main groups of employed persons were relatively modest. In summer 1995 a male worker in industry earned 73.4 per cent (monthly gross wage), a male employee in an industrial enterprise 73.4 per cent of his West German counterpart. In the trade-, banking and insurance sectors monthly gross wages of male employees were 72.9 per cent of the West German level.[35]

But it is not only material disadvantages that are the reasons for the anger of the East Germans. Mental problems, resulting from the dominance of the West Germans ('*Wessis*') in the east and the arrogant behaviour of many of them ('*Besserwessis*') against the East Germans ('*Ossis*')[36] are frustrating the East Germans just as much.

The origin of the mutual misunderstanding of East and West Germans can probably be explained by the unexpected consequences of currency union: the concept of currency union was simple and - at least for the Bonn government and more than half of the East German population who voted for this concept in March 1990 - convincing: there exists in the Federal Republic a very successful type of market economy. If one liquidates the planned economy and the communist political system in East Germany completely, and transplants instead the economic and political framework of the Federal Republic, it was thought that only a certain push - financing *(Anschubfinanzierung)* was needed for the East German economy to become immediately as attractive (to investors) and later also as efficient and successful as the economy in the West of Germany. The concept failed completely. This can be proved by two figures: originally it was thought that a transfer of 25 billion DM annually during the first years would be enough to change the East German planned economy into a flourishing market one. The money spent in the first full year after unification in the east was 130.5 billion DM.[37]

Despite the more than five times higher than expected transfer, the upswing simply did not take place. The East German economy collapsed. The original transformation pattern was then 'enriched' by two new components: the upswing had not come as expected because of the lack of managerial abilities in the East. Entrepreneurial abilities, it was argued, cannot be created *ad hoc* by courses. Though, for the first years at least, this problem was to be solved by replacing top managers in the *Treuhand* as well as in the privatized factories by West German managers. 'Manager West can be found above all in the upper management', two sociologists Peter Glotz and Klaus Ladensack, characterized the new situation in the remaining enterprises in the new *Länder* in 1995.[38] A second reason for the failure of the 'big bang' concept was identified as the inability of the East German administration to cope with the laws of the Federal Republic. Thus high ranking positions in the east German *Länder* administrations also had to be handed over to the West Germans. The same happened to the senior posts in the judiciary, which became overwhelmingly occupied by West Germans. Up to the end of 1991, 22,000 civil servants streamed into East Germany's administrations. In May 1992 their number had reached 25,000.[39] The same was happening in the political executive, where in top positions 'unable' East Germans have been replaced by 'able' West Germans, as in the universities. 'There exists no comprehensive study of employment of West German civil servants in the East German administration', writes König, 'however, it can be safely said that West Germans are represented in all administrative levels and branches and in all public ranks.' In 1991 in the Land Brandenburg the share of West Germans was 3 per cent in the lower and middle ranks, 23 per cent in the elevated ranks and over 56.1 per cent in the higher ranks of the public service. This situation is typical for the administration in the East and has not changed much since.[40]

When even this mass transfusion of West Germans into leading positions in the East did not create the conditions for an immediate upswing, the West German media, now also dominating the East, found another, the most important reason for the so far unsuccessful transformation: the average East German himself: demanding but lazy, unable and/or unwilling to fit into the demands of a modern economy and into the cooperation with a modern administration.[41]

East Germans have become more and more subordinated to West Germans at work, in offices, in politics. This will also happen in the big cities in housing, when the majority of the restitution claims are recognized in the forthcoming years. The results will be:

1. lower position of East Germans in the occupational and income hierarchies;
2. severe under-representation of them in the ownership and control of private enterprises and in the economic elite of the new *Länder*;
3. *de facto* a lower status granted to them as regional groups of Germans.

If the process of economic destruction and subsequent increasing social dependence on West German payments and the domination of West Germans in the East German economic and political spheres goes on unabated then the development of a distinct society in the East instead of the proposed integration seems unavoidable. This will be a society of second-class Germans, separated from the West Germans by class, economic status, power and (with local exclusions like Berlin, Leipzig and Dresden) also regional economic grievances unknown to their countrymen in the West.

The West German politicians, especially the governing coalition, have up to now not analysed the economic and social roots of the new division of the Germans. What they wished to avoid were political consequences, endangering their political position and election chances. They successfully bound the East German deputies to the *Bundestag*, mostly belonging to 'united' parties, in the parliamentary party discipline. The East German deputies have to bow to the aims of the (West German) majority. Since there had been no proper political counterparts in the West who could take over this disciplinary action - as the former communists and the representatives of the civic movements of 1989 - the media did their utmost to discredit these minority groups, especially the former communists, bringing them arbitrarily into connection with the *Stasi*, the former East German secret service.[42]

The appearance of a political leadership in the East which would represent the different, often contrary to the West Germans, interests of the East German population, has also been prevented on the *Länder* level. Representatives who could become influential leaders by their stand on Western democracy as well as certain Eastern values like solidarity, e.g. the president of Humboldt-University, Fink, the Prime Minister of Land Brandenburg, Stolpe, the Minister of Interior in the de Maiziere government, Diestel, and the Prime Minister of the GDR during the revolution, Modrow, have all been victims of a media campaigns in McCarthy style with the aim to discredit them as *Stasi* spies, political adventurers or criminals.[43]

The obvious - or at least in the minds of many East Germans obvious - misuse of parliamentary democracy, a free press and the judiciary is beginning to discredit parliamentary democracy as well as the constitutional foundations of the rule of law (*Rechtsstaatlichkeit*). 'Between 1990 and 1995 the expectations for improvements in the conditions have been lowered dramatically. At the same time the share of those with negative expectations rose remarkably', summarized sociologists their findings six years after unification.[44]

Such results are not surprising, despite the euphoria of the majority of East Germans about parliamentary democracy and the market economy of the West German style in the months preceding unification, only two years ago. The East German realities appear to prove more the validity of the Marxist thesis of class struggle than the appearance of a democratic classless society. In the case of existential problems (e.g. the closure of key enterprises, which endanger the employment in a whole town or region) the affected are aware that it will not be helpful to turn to their regional deputies of the Federal Diet with their grievances, or to write petitions to the Chancellor in Bonn. Success in preventing - at least temporarily - factory closures or improving the sales contracts of *Treuhand* (as far as the number of temporarily guaranteed jobs is concerned) have been those who demonstrated in the streets, occupied the plants or stopped the traffic on nearby streets and railway lines, as for instance the workforce of *Zeiss Jena*, of *Schwermaschinenbau Lauchhammer*, of *Walzwerk Finow* and *EKO Eisenhüttenstadt*, and above all the hunger-strikers of the potash pit in the Thuringian village of Bischofferode. During their first regional meeting the shop stewards (*Betriebsäte*) of the five *Länder* argued that they had reached limited successes in the past only when they used 'not just legal means' (*quasi regelwidrige Mittel*).[45]

When East Germans felt - mostly unjustified - that foreigners (former GDR guest-workers from Vietnam and Mozambique or persons from other third-world countries, seeking political asylum) were endangering the remaining jobs, they learned that noting right-wing youth groups were much more successful in driving foreigners away or stopping their influx in the communities than appeals of the inhabitants to the elected local administration. This explains why the 'normal citizen' applauded violent youth groups as in the case of the mining town of Hoyerswerda, and the city port of Rostock, where the hitherto most serious riots in the East took place.[46]

Thus it seems obvious that if the channels of political communication between the East German population and the Bonn government, indeed between East and West Germans, are blocked further, grievances might be expressed perhaps less skilfully, but more effectively by non-parliamentary, including violent means.[47] This would not only put into question the role of politicians, against whom distrust and dismay are broadly spread under the East Germans,[48] but would also threaten the whole system of parliamentary democracy.

The attempts to create an 'East German party' or 'East German movement' to correct the mistakes of both unification treaties of 1990 and defend East German interests more efficiently against West German domination, which at first occurred in December 1991 and became stronger in June 1992 can be judged from this point of view a positive response, because resistance may be channelled in a democratic way. Embarrassing for the 'united parties', the former communists benefited from the lack of political representation of the East Germans on federal level. In the federal election of autumn 1994 it became obvious that an increasing part of East Germans believes that only the PDS (Party of Democratic Socialism) is able to act as representation of East German regional interests. In the new *Länder* the PDS got 11.8 per cent of the votes cast in the first elections after the unification of Germany in autumn 1990, but 19.8 per cent four years later. Though the PDS is not a member of one of the governing coalitions in the East, at least one of the *Länder* governments (Sachsen-Anhalt) depends on the goodwill of the PDS deputies in the local parliament.[49] Politically these movements only confirm what economically and socially is obvious: 'The signs of stagnation in the process of German unification cannot be overlooked', wrote Karl Feldmeyer, a commentator of the famous *Frankfurter Zeitung* in August 1996, 'the question whether the division of the Germans in one people of the "GDR" and in one of the "FRG" will happen belatedly ... occupies also the minds of those to whom the unity of the nation means a lot.'[50]

Notes

1 FRG taken as 100 per cent, the estimates were (1985) 54 per cent by the United Nations and (also 1986) the World Bank, 50 per cent (1983) by *'Deutsches Wirtschaftsinstitut'* (DIW) and 48 per cent by a well known based research institution. UN (1988) *International Comparison to Gross Domestic Product in Europe 1985*, New York, p. 4; Collier, I.L. (1985), 'The Estimation of Gross Domestic Product and its Growth Rate for the German Democratic Republic', *World Bank Staff Working Papers* No. 773, Washington; Cornelsen, D. and Kirner, W., 'Zum Produktivitätsvergleich Bundesrepublik - DDR', in: *DIW-Wochenbericht* 14/90, p. 172; (1986), 'Research Project on National Income in East-Central Europe'. Occasional Paper Nos. 90-94. L.W. International Financial Research Inc. New York. All calculations are based mainly on data of the GDR Statistical Office. These were checked by the Staff Federal Statistical Office after unification and found realistic with only minor exclusions. Hölder E. (1991), 'Statement des Präsidenten des Statistischen Bundesamtes' *DDR-Statistik, Schein und Wirklichkeit.* Wiesbaden, p. 8.

2 (1990), *Statistisches Jahrbuch der Deutschen Demokratischen Republik 1990*, Berlin, p. 110

3 Görzig, B. and Gornig, M. (1991), 'Produktivität und Wettbewerbsfähigkeit in der Wirtschaft der DDR', in: DIW. *Beiträge zur Strukturforschung*, vol. 121, Berlin, p. 14.

4 Thaysen, U. (1990), *Der Rund Tisch oder Wo blieb das Volk?* Opladen, p. 82-98; Luft, C. (1991), *Zwischen Wende und Ende*, Berlin, p. 147-49; Arnold, K.H. (1990), *Die ersten hundert Tage des Hans Modrow*, Berlin, p. 94; Roesler, J. 'Between Self-Determination and Unification: East Germans from October 1989 to October 1990', in: *German History*, London, p. 167-68.

5 This was assured by both heads of governments to the people of East Germany when they signed the treaty about the currency union on 19 May 1990.(1990), *Der Staatsvertrag, Grundlage der deutschen Einheit*, Berlin/Bonn, pp. 7, 9.

6 'Zur wirtschaftlichen und sozialen Lage in den ostdeutschen Ländern', in: *WSI-Mitteilungen.* Cologne, 11/1990, p. 708.

7 *Wirtschaft und Statistik*, Wiesbaden, 9/90, p. 376.

8 (1991), *Produktion und Produktionsfaktoren in Ostdeutschland.* Dokumentation des DIW, Berlin, p. 28.

9 Süß, W. 'Geschichte der Treuhand. Eine Behörde verkauft die ostdeutsche Volkswirtschaft', in: *Das Parlament*, Bonn, 13/1992, p. 13.

10 More positive: Buck, H.F. (1991), *Von der staatlichen*

Kommandowirtschaft der DDR zur sozialen Marktwirtschaft des vereinten Deutschland, Düsseldorf, p. 39-51. More negative: Suhr, H. (1991), *Der Treuhandskandal*, Frankfurt/Main. Semi official: (1991), *Sachverständigenrat zur Begutachtung der gesamtwirtschaftlichen Entwicklung: Marktwirtschaftlichen Kurs halten. Zur Wirtschaftspolitik für die neuen Bundesländer*, Sondergutachten, p. 14-17.

11 (1990), 'Vertrag zwischen der Bundesrepublik Deutschland und der Deutschen Demokratischen Republik über die Herstellung der Einheit Deutschlands (Einigungsvertrag)'. Bonn, *Bundesgesetzblatt* No. 104, p. 888.

12 'The Situation of the World Economy and the German Economy in the Spring of 1992', in: *Ifo Digest* 2 (1992), p. 16. *Neues Deutschland*, May 5, 1995.

13 Görzig, B. (1992), 'Productivity Comparisons: East versus West Germany'. DIW-paper, Berlin, p. 7.

14 Bundesbank, *Monthly Report*, Frankfurt/Main, 12 (1994), p. 84; Data recently published by the Institut für Wirtschaftsforschung, Halle (IWH), in: *Der Tagesspiegel*, September 23, 1996

15 Modrow, H. (1989), 'Regierungserklärung', in: *Neues Deutschland*, Berlin, November 18/19, p. 3-4.

16 *Statistisches Jahrbuch der DDR 1955*, Berlin (1956), p. 119; 1959. Berlin (1960), p. 207, 242. Covert unemployment was not reported. In May 1990 two West German research institutes (Ifo-Institut, München and Institut für Angewandte Wirtschaftsforschung, Berlin made estimates about the number of covert unemployed. They were able to make full use of the data of the East German Statistical Office. Using several different definitions, the institutes arrived at around 20 per cent. The possible maximum was around 30 per cent. *Neues Deutschland*, August 20, 1991.)

17 *Gesetzblatt der DDR 1990*, no. 18, p. 161; no. 11, p. 83; no. 18, p. 161.

18 Lothar de Maiziere: 'Regierungserklärung', in: *Neues Deutschland*, April 20, p. 5.

19 Janoski, T. (1990), *The Political Economy of Unemployment. Active Labor Market Policy in West Germany and the United States*, Berkeley, p. 4-6.

20 Belwe, K. (1991), *Psycho-soziale Befindlichkeit der Menschen in den neuen Bundesländern nach der Wende im Herbst 1989*, Bonn, p.7.

21 Kurbjuweit, D. 'Abschied von der reinen Lehre' in: *Die Zeit*, 20/1991, p. 27.

22 Buck, H.F. (1991), *Von der staatlichen Kommandowirtschaft der DDR zur sozialen Marktwirtschaft des vereinten Deutschland*. Düsseldorf, p. 74.

23 Jörg Roesler, 'Arbeitslosigkeit in den neuen Bundesländern - Umfang,

Ursachen, Befindlichkeiten und Bewältigungstrategien', in: *Rissener Rundbrief*, 5/1991, p. 133-35.

24 *Frankfurter Rundschau*, Frankfurt/Main, February 13, 1991.

25 Kurbjuweit, p. 27.

26 *Frankfurter Allgemeine Zeitung*, January 8, 1991.

27 Kurbjuweit, p. 27.

28 *Ibid.*

29 *Frankfurter Allgemeine Zeitung.* January 9, 1992.

30 *Frankfurter Allgemeine Zeitung*, February 6, 1992; *Der Tagesspiegel*, July 29, 1996; *ibid.* August 6, 1996; *Das Parlament*, 35 (1995), p. 6.

31 *Wirtschaft und Statistik*, 4/1992, p. 189; *Das Parlament*, Bonn, 22-23/1992, p. 7; *Wirtschaftswoche*, Berlin, 12/1992, p. 9; *Neues Deutschland*, Berlin, June 6, 1992. In the McKinsey report, ordered by the Federal government in spring 1991 and kept secret at that time, regional unemployment quotas up to 70 per cent were envisaged for the future. (McKinsey & Company, Überlegungen zur kurzfristigen Stabilisierung und langfristigen Steigerung der Wirtschaftskraft in den neuen Bundesländern, Düsseldorf/München, April 1991, p. 11.). Querschnittsgruppe 'Deutsche Einheit' der SPD-Bundestagsfraktion, 'Jahresarbeitsmarktbericht 1995/6 (Kurzfassung)', in: *Neues Deutschland*, April 2, 1996; Steininger, M., 'Der Osten am Tropf', in *ibid.*, September 26, 1996; *Berliner Zeitung*, September 6, 1996; *Der Tagesspiegel*, September 6, 1996.

32 Peter P. & Headey, B. & Habich, R. 'Einkommensentwicklung der privaten Haushalte in Ostdeutschland', in: *Deutschlandarchiv*, Cologne, 3/1992, p. 298-303; *The Situation of the World Economy*, p. 18. 'Die Wachstumsaussichten Ostdeutschlands', in: Bank Gesellschaft Berlin: *Wirtschaftsreport*, 2/1995, p. 6; *Der Tagesspiegel*, August 26, 1996.

33 *The Situation of the World Economy*, p. 17; Hall, J., Ludwig, U., 'German unification and the "market adoption" hypothesis', in: *Cambridge Journal of Economics*, 19/1995, p. 406; IWH: 'Die Lage der Weltwirtschaft und der deutschen Wirtschaft im Herbst 1995', in: *Wirtschaft und Wandel*, 14/1995, p. 25; Steinitz, K., 'Hohe Löhne - Grundübel ostdeutscher Wirtschaft?' in: *Neues Deutschland*, July 27, 1996.

34 Stingel, R. 'Jammernde Gewinner. Deutsche Einheit - Bilanz nach einem Jahr' in: *Wirtschaftswoche*, 40/1991, pp. 46-47; Heckel, M., Weidendeld, U., Canibol, H.P. 'Hirten und Wölfe. Die Deutschen sind zerstrittener denn je' in: *Wirtschaftswoche*, 15/1992, pp. 12-20.

35 Sozialreport: 'Durchschnittseinkommen Ost-West', *Neues Deutschland*, August 9, 1991; 'Sozialreport: Einkommen im Ost-West-Vergleich in ausgewählten Tarifbereichen', in: *Neues Deutschland*, May 15, 1992; *Das Parlament*, 8-9/1996, p. 11; *Neues Deutschland*, September 5, 1996.

36 Belwe, K., p. 17-18. In an opinion poll in Berlin was asked, what does hinder most the coming together of Berliners in East and West: 17 per cent of east Berliners named the different incomes, 16 per cent the 'arrogance of the west Berliners'. (*Neues Deutschland*, December 10, 1991).

37 The first sum was named in an expert report, ordered by Chancellor Kohl's office (Bundeskanzleramt) in March 1990 at the University of Cologne. (Hans Willgerodt, Barbara Dluhosch, Malte Krüger: Gutachten: Vorteile der wirtschaftlichen Einheit Deutschlands, Cologne 1990, p. 20). For the second sum: *The situation of the world economy*, p. 17.

38 The East German managers have to be replaced up to 90 per cent according to the leading *Treuhand* personal manager Alexander Koch. Fifteen thousand 'imports' would be necessary for the 7,500 at October 1991 not yet privatized *Treuhand* enterprises, according to a consulting agency for personnel (*Frankfurther Allgemeine Zeitung*, October 31, 1991). In the same direction argue Schwenn and Thierse (Schwenn, K. 'Ostdeutschland braucht Manager', *ibid.*, December 12, 1991; Thierse, W. 'Die alten Seilschaften in der neuen Freiheit', *ibid.*, November 27, 1991). Against this opinion: Koch T. 'Alte Kader für die neue Zeit', in: *Die Zeit*, 46/1991, p. 27-29; Glotz, P. & Ladensack, K. 'Strukturwandel im Management ostdeutscher Unternehmen', in: *Arbeit und Arbeitsrecht*, 9/1995, p. 292.

39 *Das Parlament*, 5/1992, p. 5. In May 1992 according to the Chancellor's office 15,000 of the civil servants, 'lent' to the eastern *'Länder'* had worked originally in the Federal offices, 8,000 in the west German *'Länder'* and 2,000 in town administrations. (*Tageszeitung*, Berlin, June 11, 1992).

40 König, K., Bureaucratic Integration by Elite Transfer: The Case of the Former GDR, in: *Governance*, Cambridge, MA, USA, 3/1993, p. 391.

41 Belwe, K. 'Innere Einigung schwieriger als erwartet', in *Das Parlament*, 47/1991, p. 11; Wolfgang Jantzen, 'Die psychische Situation der Ostdeutschen', in: *Neues Deutschland*, January 25/26, 1992.

42 The misuse of the *Stasi* files by the media was repeatedly criticized. 'The discussion of the files becomes more and more one-sided on the person and depends more and more on the political role (*'Prominenz'*) the person named in the files plays at present'. (*Frankfurter Rundschau*, June 13, 1992)

43 See especially the witch hunt of the only Social Democrat under the prime ministers of the five *Länder*, Stolpe, initiated by the journal *Der Spiegel* (*Der Spiegel*, 8/1992. p. 24-33). A renewal of the attack on the Brandenburg Prime Minister, re-elected in 1994 with an overwhelming majority, was started with 'fresh facts' by *Der Spiegel* in September 1996, cf. Oschmann, R., 'Stolpe und der kalte Krieg' in: *Neues Deutschland*, September 25, 1996.

44 Priller, E., 'Demokratieentwicklung und gesellsschaftliche Mitwirkung', in: Winkler, G. (ed.), (1996), *Sozialreport Daten und Fakten zur sozialen Lage in den neuen Bundesländern*, Berlin, p. 338.

45 *Neues Deutschland*, June 20/21, 1992; June 22, 1992. In a secret expert report ordered by the Bonn government, the experts are warning of the consequences of 'public pressure', which could lead to the fact, 'that in future closures take place only there, where it does not endanger the regional political peace'. (McKinsey, *Überlegungen zur kurzfirstigen Stabilisierung*, p. 18); see also Blaschke, R., 'Bischofferode als eine Schockterapie' in: *Neues Deutschland*, August 30/31, 1993.

46 Hoyerswerda belongs to the regions with the highest percentage of unemployment in *Land* Brandenburg. (*Berliner Zeitung*. Berlin, November 11, 1991); Rostock is the biggest city in Mecklenburg-Vorpommern, the *Land* with the highest unemployment in Germany.

47 The McKinsey expert report assessed 'potential social unrest in the new '*Bundesländer*' endanger the political climate in the whole of Germany'. (*Überlegungen zur kurzfirstigen Stabilisierung*, p. 13)

48 This is to be seen in the low turnout to elections in all new *Länder* since unification. It became especially obvious in East Berlin, where only 57.4 per cent of the electorate took part in the May 1992 elections, compared with 80.8 per cent in September 1990. (*Die Zeit*, 16/1992, p. 16: *Neues Deutschland*, May 26, 1992.)

49 In November such a party was founded in East Berlin by representatives of small business (*Mittelstand*), disappointed with the (West) Berlin government economic policy. (*Novembers Deutschland*, 30/ December 1, 1991). In May 1992 the idea of a special East German party was initiated again by the former Interior Minister of the last GDR government H. Diestel. (Bender, P.: 'Zwei, drei, viele Ostparteien. Plädoyer für eine Rebellion der Ostdeutschen', in: *Wochenpost*, 25/1991, p. 4.). See also German Information Centre, (1994) 'The October 16, 1994 Bundestag Election and Three State Elections in the Federal Republic of Germany', New York; Lang, J.P. & Moreau, P. & Neu, V. (1994) ... *auferstanden aus Ruinen ...? Die PDS nach dem Super-Wahljahr 1994*, St. Augustin, pp. 15-22.

50 Feldmeyer, K., 'Deutschlandpolitik ist nicht zu Ende', in: *Frankfurter Allgemeine Zeitung*, August 13, 1996.

CHAPTER EIGHT

From Interwar Stagnation to Postwar Prosperity: Austria's Reconstruction after 1945

Fritz Weber

Gottfried Haberler once characterized the economic development of Austria after 1918 as a 'mirror picture of the world economy'.[1] But this is true only in a very general sense: during the twentieth century, Austria has twice been right in the epicentre of political earthquakes, and her economy has twice been hit by cataclysmic structural shocks caused by these political events: the break-down of great empires at the end of lost wars.

The repercussions of the downfall of the Habsburg Monarchy were to be felt for decades. In autumn 1918, an economic *Großraum* with its historically grown regional division of labour fell apart, and the economy of the new small state could never be adjusted to its new environment. Neither could it gain a structural equilibrium within the neo-mercantilist world of the 1920s, nor was it able to recover from the Great Depression of 1929. The 1930s proved to be, following the Austrian economist Kurt W. Rothschild, a time of 'retrogressive adjustment' marked by a general shrinking which affected above all the 'overcrowded and maladjusted branches'.[2]

The second structural blow occurred in 1945, after Austria had been part of the German *Reich* for seven years. At the end of the Nazi period the state of the Austrian economy seemed - at first sight - even worse than after the First World War: especially in the eastern parts of the country infrastructure, buildings and industrial plants had been heavily hit by Allied bombardments. Since prices had been frozen since 1938, there was an 'enormous monetary cloud hanging above an economy stripped of goods', as an Austrian contemporary economist put it.[3] In other words, there was an acute danger of hyper-inflation, which could easily have surpassed the dimensions of the period 1918-22, when the Austrian crown had been devalued to a 14.400th part of its gold value.

Nevertheless the problems of economic reconstruction were overcome astonishingly fast: during the interwar years Austria's GNP had touched the prewar level (1913) only for a short period (1928-30). The shock waves of this experience were still present after 1945, when economic experts and planners stared spellbound at the 1913 and 1937 figures as the ultimate limit to be reached. However, to their surprise, the GNP left behind both the 1937 and 1913 level already in 1949; only foreign trade and agriculture lagged behind reaching the 1913 level in the mid-1950s. In 1960 economic activity had almost doubled as against 1913. (See Figure 8.1)

Figure 8.1 Real growth of GNP in Austria, 1913-82

After 1945, the Austrian growth rates lay well above the overall European trend, whereas the interwar years had turned out relatively badly (see Table 8.1). The general explanations for the brilliant performance of the postwar economy can be taken for granted: the Schumpeterian argument related to the long waves of the business cycle, Svennilson's idea of a non-utilized growth potential inherited from the interwar period, a stable international monetary system, the abolition of trade barriers, and, last but not least, the Keynesian revolution. They need not be repeated here. What remains to be done is to depict the specific Austrian path of development. This will be the subject of this essay.

Table 8.1 Austrian and international economic growth 1913-74 (compound growth rates of GDP)

Period	Average of European OECD countries	Austria
1913-1937*	1.2**	- 0.4
1953-1962	4.8	6.3
1962-1967	4.4	4.3
1967-1974	4.6	5.2

* Growth per head; for the following periods: real growth
** 1913-1938
OECD - Organization for Economic Organization and Development

Sources: Österreichs Volkseinkommen 1913-1963. Monatsberichte des WIFO, 14. Vienna 1965, p. 14; Butschek, (1985) *Die österreichische Wirtschaft im 20* Jahrhundert, (Stuttgart-Vienna) pp. 119, 129, 144. Special issue.

1. Destruction or modernization? The long-run consequences of the Nazi period

Some figures may illustrate the disastrous economic scenario left to the Austrians after the war. Fighting and exhaustion of the soil considerably lowered the crop yield during the first postwar year.[4] Many industrial plants had been damaged. In Lower Austria 140 mills had been totally destroyed, 120 had been heavily hit. Although the degree of destruction cannot be exactly calculated - the available figures also take into account the effects of postwar dismantling in the French and Soviet occupation zones - the overall loss of machinery caused by war activities can be assessed as at least 30 per cent of the 1944 stock.[5]

The greatest damages occurred - as in other countries affected by the war - in infrastructure and housing. One -third of the Austrian railway network was out of order; six per cent of all railway bridges - including all the connections over the Danube river - were impassable. At the end of 1946 the number of locomotives ready for service reached only 50 per cent of the 1937 total.[6]

Havoc in private and public buildings was great. A tenth of the housing stock had been destroyed.[7]

The demographic statistics show - despite the blood letting in battle fields - a surplus because of the immigration of so-called 'displaced persons' from Eastern Europe. However, 150,000 disabled persons were only fit for limited service, and Austrian prisoners of war were only gradually allowed to return from the Soviet Union; there was a great scarcity of skilled workers during the initial stage of reconstruction.

The supposed dimensions of the loss of national wealth resulting from war damages and dismantling have occupied both the energies and fantasies of economists. According to an early calculation of the Austrian Institute for Economic Research (WIFO - Österreichisches Institut für Wirtschaftsforschung) the losses amounted to about one third of the overall capital stock. Angus Maddison reported a loss of 16 per cent, referring to the Austrian economist Anton Kausel.[8] More recent historical investigations have offered a much brighter view: Felix Butschek considers that destruction and increment counterbalanced each other; Norbert Schausberger's opinion, based on qualitative research, is of an even more optimistic character.[9]

If we ignore dismantling, the destruction of wealth was more than outweighed by investments of German enterprises and the Nazi state after the *Anschluß* of 1938 (see Table 8.4). The occupation was accompanied by a radical modernization of the Austrian economy, albeit by a *dependent modernization of a quasi-colonial type*, subordinated to the needs and wants of the German war economy. Nevertheless, the bulk of these investments proved to be valuable for the postwar development, too.

German investments concentrated upon branches of *strategic* importance, like the development of water power stations in the Alpine regions, the intensification of oil extraction in the Marchfeld (near Vienna) and, above all, the foundation of new enterprises (or the extension of the existing ones) in the investment goods and war industries. The number of machine tools within these *strategic* branches was increased at a rate of more than 50 per cent between December 1937 and April 1945 (see Table 8.4). The production of electricity rose from 2.890 million kWh (1938) to 5.980 (1944), that is about 100 per cent. Eighteen big water power stations were initiated after 1938, of which, however, only six could be completed before the end of the war. The most impressive figure concerns oil extraction, which was extended from 30,000 tons before the war to 1.2 million in 1944.

Industrial formations of importance were the aluminium works at Ranshofen, the pulp mill at Lenzing, the huge metallurgical plant of the Hermann Göring Works at Linz, all of them situated in Upper Austria, and the steelworks at Krems (Lower Austria) and at Liezen (Styria). Investments of that kind were to increase the industrial weight of the western parts of Austria *in the long run*, since those *Länder* (provinces) were granted special favours *after* the war, too, receiving the greater share of the counterpart funds of the ERP (European Recovery Program). Although Lower Austria was still *the* industrial heart of the country, it received only 6 per cent of the ERP money until the end of 1953, whereas the shares of Carinthia, Salzburg, Upper Austria and Styria varied between 11 and 21 per cent.[10]

Although the plants established or initiated during the war years were reactivated and completed after 1945, the regional (see Table 8.2) as well as

Tale 8.2 Share of western and eastern provinces in industrial employment (as a percentage of overall industrial employment), 1937 and 1947

Zone	September 1937	September 1947
Eastern Austria *	60.4	48.6
Western Austria **	39.6	51.4

*   Vienna, Lower Austria, Styria, Burgenland.
**   Upper Austria, Salzburg, Carinthia, Tyrol, Vorarlberg.

Source: Niederösterreich an der Arbeit. Entwicklung und Leistung der gewerblichen Wirstschaft des Landes, Horn 1948, p. 167.

structural changes (see Table 8.3) of the Nazi period were halted during the period of reconstruction. (By way of contrast, during the inter-war period the secular economic crisis had brought forth a continuous decline in the employment of the investment goods sector.)

The support of the structural war-time changes was not that 'natural' process it would seem by hindsight: Many of the plants in question were in a semi-finished state, many of them had been partially destroyed during the war and, last, but not least, those situated in the regions liberated by the Red Army had to endure heavy dismantling before being reconstructed.[11] Table 8.4 indicates quite clearly the extent of Soviet dismantling. Another figure may show the regional difference: whereas the machine building industry lost 70 per cent of its capacity in Vienna and Lower Austria, it maintained 70 per cent in the western parts of the country.[12] The industrial regions of Styria (which had been initially occupied by the Red Army) seem to have suffered a fate similar to that of Lower Austria.[13]

Dismantling of 'German foreign assets' (for which the Potsdam Agreement created the legal basis) considerably hindered economic reconstruction during the immediate postwar period, since the gaps within the productive apparatus existed just in those sectors strategic to reconstruction. To cite two examples: since all the Austrian non-ferrous metal works had been dismantled, aluminium could only be rolled at steel rolling mills, which meant a considerable reduction in the quality of goods. The capacity of the iron-working industry was badly hit by the removal of the modern rolling train of the Alpine works at Donawitz (Styria). The old system, ready for scrapping, had to be reassembled, before the Alpine works were able to start meeting the most urgent demand in March 1946.[14]

Table 8.3 Distribution of employment within Austrian industry according to branches, 1902-70 (as %)

Sector	1902	1920-22*	1930*	1938	1954	1970
Investment goods industry	44.7	56.4	49.2	46.6	58.6	63.5
Consumer goods industry	55.3	43.6	50.8	53.4	41.4	36.5

* Only blue-collar workers.

Sources: Statistische Nachrichten, Jg. 1925, p. 49; *Wirtschaftsstatistisches Jahrbuch* 1930/31, pp. 142-143; Nemschak, *Zehn Jahre,* p. 65; Koren, S. 'Die Industrialisierung Österreichs' in: Weber, W. (ed.), *op. cit.,* vol. 1, p. 265.

Table 8.4 Machinery stock of strategic sectors* of Austrian industry, 1937-46 (in units)

	December 1937	April 1945	January 1946
	60,700	92,200	49,600
+/- (as % against 1937)		+ 51.9%	- 18.3%
January 1946 (as % against December 1937			81.7

* As defined above: war and investment goods industries.

Source: Monatsberichte des WIFO , 1-3/1947, p. 29.

2. The Achilles heel of Reconstruction: Infrastructure, raw material and the food deficit

Most of the devastating results of dismantling were not felt immediately after the war; in 1945/46 one could - with the exception of coal mining or extraction of magnesite - not speak of industrial 'production' in the narrow sense of the word. The majority of the workforce was still occupied by repairs to buildings, machinery, means of transportation, and by what we could call removing the ruins of war.

Besides dismantling and war damages the lack of fuel and the almost complete destitution from lack of raw materials and semi-finished goods, which could not be replaced, were the main problems of restarting industrial production. The very key, however, to open the door for economic reconstruction lay in the reorganization of the transport system and of the infrastructure as a whole. This was neither a specific Austrian nor a mere national problem.[15] Restarting transportation on a European scale can be regarded as the crucial economic question of 1945 Europe.

Similar to Germany, the initial problems of the Austrian transport system were not mere 'technical' ones. The recovery of inland trade was further hindered and delayed by a phenomenon which the Austrian WIFO called the 'latent trade war' between the occupation zones, especially between the western provinces and the Soviet occupied area.[16] Well into 1946, the inner-Austrian trade between East and West was confined to barter shipments, which discriminated against the eastern regions, which had hardly anything to offer in compensation for 'import' goods. To quote an example: in autumn 1945 Upper Austria exchanged sodium carbonate against crude glass from Czechoslovakia, at a time when the Lower Austrian glass industry was suffering from an acute scarcity of soda.[17]

The eastern parts of the country were in a worse situation, not only as concerns war damages and dismantling. There was a greater shortage of electricity, because the power lines to the Alpine regions were broken and most of the power stations were dependent on coal; railway transport, too, was hampered by severe lack of fuel, whereas electrified lines were located in the Alpine provinces.

Lower Austria, the Burgenland and, in particular, Vienna were also underprivileged in the realm of nutrition. In May 1945, the official daily ration of a Viennese citizen amounted to 350 calories; during the following months it was increased to 800. Yet in autumn 1948, when additional food imports were provided by the Marshall Plan, only a 2100 calories ration could be made available to the Austrian population.[18]

Even during the following years, Austria proved to be unable to live on her own food resources. In the beginning, foodstuffs were supplied by the Allied Powers in 1946-47, by UNRRA (United Nations Relief and Rehabilitation Administration) 1947 and later mainly by the USA. Until the end of 1949 almost two thirds of the ERP aid granted to Austria consisted of foodstuffs.

The significance of foreign relief can be seen from Table 8.5. (In 1947, the share of foodstuffs procured from abroad was even greater.)

Table 8.5 Sources of foodstuffs distributed among Austrian
non-agrarian population in 1946 (%)

Austrian agriculture	39%
Commercial imports	1%
UNRRA	60%

Source: Rothschild, *Austrian Economy*, p. 30.

Until mid-1947 Austria's supply of foodstuffs (and therewith the maintenance of social peace) repeatedly hung by the notorious silk thread.[19] Famine led to a decrease in productivity in industry and mining and provoked so-called 'calorie strikes'. Moreover, tensions between the industrial and agricultural population stiffened, since many scarce goods appeared only on the black market.

The supply of coal and raw materials was hampered mainly by the languishing international as well as national transport system. Pit-coal and other important imports could not reach Austria, whereas the country had nothing to offer to foreigners *because* of the lack of transport facilities, fuel and raw materials; and there were only a few precious primary goods like magnesite, which could be sold abroad.[20]

As in other European countries all those difficulties reached their critical peak in winter 1946/47, when a catastrophic shortage of energy threatened to wreck all the progress already made.[21] Austria was shaken by a pre-industrial crisis caused by the inclemency of nature: a dry summer and a severe winter, which both disabled the water power stations of the country.

During the first months of 1947 rail transport came to a standstill; the only blast-furnace in service at the Alpine Montan-Gesellschaft had to be shut down as well as energy-consuming production of aluminium at Ranshofen which had just been reactivated. Subsequently several industries were put out of operation. But finally the crisis was overcome by planned economic measures: the Austrian authorities had prepared an emergency plan which provided measures for reactivating industry in case of an energy breakdown and ensured the gradual resumption of production starting with the iron and steel industry.[22]

After the energy crisis of 1947 had been overcome, the path of economic recovery was soon resumed. Foreign trade, too, which in 1946 - excluding relief shipments - had reached only 8 per cent of the 1937 volume, was gradually restored to life. The overwhelming part of frontier crossing transactions, however, was not listed in the books. Austria's external trade equilibrium, as was indicated by foreign trade statistics, was a mere fiction: in 1946, commercial imports of foodstuffs amounted to about $2 million (US); the overall import figure, however, was 125 million, 123 million of which did not show up, because they concerned relief goods. Without foreign assistance Austria would not have been able to cover her external trade deficit in the most crucial years of reconstruction (see Table 8.6).

Table 8.6 Austria's real balance of trade and foreign aid,
1946–49 (in US$m)

Year	Imports	Exports	Foreign trade deficit	Share of relief in imports
1946	228.1*	21.9	206.2*	200.0**
1947	312.0	90.7	221.3	225.4
1948	501.7	207.1	294.6	304.9
1949	594.2	289.1	301.1	313.4

*   Calculation following the statement of Rothschild.
**   Estimate of Nemschak for 1945-46.

Sources: Zehn Jahre ERP, p. 91; Nemschak, *Zehn Jahre*, p. 23; Rothschild, *Austrian Economy*, p. 32.

3. The political economy of reconstruction:
Social partnership, nationalization and full employment

As already mentioned, one of the most acute dangers after the breakdown of the Nazi system was suppressed inflation: while - due to war prize regulations - prices had been kept at the 1938 level, money supply had been increased six-fold.[23] Moreover, after the war *Reichsmark* notes were pouring into Austria, and the quantity of money in circulation was further increased by the Allied occupation troops printing bank notes for their own purpose.

The continuation of the war regulations and the declaration of a price and wage freeze by the Allied Powers could not prevent inflation, as Figure 8.2 indicates, which shows the enormous gap between official and black market prices. The 'money cloud' therefore had to be reduced by several steps between 1945 and 1947; the *Schaltergesetz* of July 1945, and the *Schillinggesetz* of November 1947.

In place of an uncontrolled inflation Austria passed through a period of 'officially controlled inflation'.[24] Between 1947 and 1951 five so-called *Lohn-Preis-Abkommen* (wage-price-agreements) were bargained under patronage of the government by the trade unions and the representatives of entrepreneurial and agrarian interests. The effects of the agreements can also be seen in Figure 8.2. The aim of the agreements was to regulate the inflationary impulses which could have emanated from both wages and agrarian prices. Their *political* objective was to maintain social peace in a crucial period of reconstruction by levelling the differential between high and low wages and by nipping in the bud uncontrolled local wage campaigns. The economic philosophy behind them was that wages should lag behind prices, thus enabling a high rate of investment by forced saving.[25]

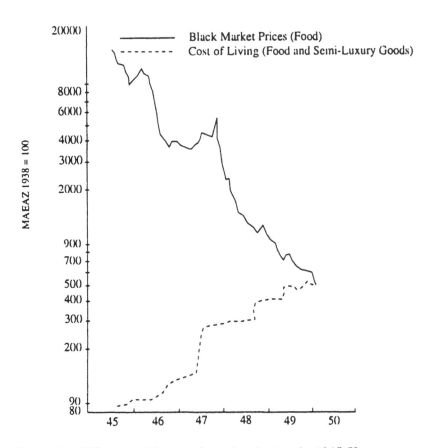

Figure 8.2 Official and black market prices in Austria, 1945-50

Why did the trade unions (and the majority of the Austrian working class) voluntarily agree to such a strategy? The social democratic oriented trade union leaders defended their policy mainly with reference to interwar experience. During the inflationary period following the First World War, the trade unions had succeeded in pushing through a sliding wage scale, i.e. the automatic adaptation of wages to increased prices. In hindsight that offensive kind of wage policy was interpreted as failure, because it had contributed to hyper-inflation and had led to the Geneva reform, a synonym for political and social counter-revolution, and, ultimately, to the victory of Austro-fascism in 1933/34.[26] Moreover, the trade union leaders did the utmost to avoid what they believed inflationary chaos, which might provoke the Communists 'to fish in troubled waters'.[27]

After the Second World War a general learning process from the past brought together the former enemies of the First Austrian Republic. This was rendered possible by a unique overall political situation, characterized not only by the beginning of the Cold War (with Austria at the front line of the events) but also by the traumatic memory of mass unemployment of the 1930s, and - no less - by the fact that the Nazi system in Austria had not been overcome by a mass movement, but by the Allied armies.

In 1918/19 *workers councils* had challenged the civil order; in 1945 the *Revolution der Hofräte*[28] (revolution of the privy councillors) re-established orderly circumstances. The Austrian working class concentrated on reactivating production and delegated political power to the social democratic leaders. The 'great' political and economic post-1945 design was to be sketched by 'bureaucratic' institutions.

There was hardly any important decision of the immediate postwar era, which would not have been legitimated by referring to the historical lessons of the interwar period. This was also true for the realm of economics: Keynesianism was not a 'pure' theory but something like a theoretical condensate of practical consequences, which the politicians anyhow were ready to draw from the stagnation of the 1930s.[29] In Austria, in contrast to Western Germany, the trauma of mass unemployment was probably much deeper than that of hyper-inflation.

Other cornerstones of the 'political economy of reconstruction' were the willingness to co-operate in politics (Great Coalition governments of 1945-1966, 1945-47 including also the Communist Party) as well as in social matters (social partnership, starting at the latest with the wage-price-agreements), and the wholehearted certainty that Austria was an economically viable country.[30] Even concerning planning and nationalization there was a fundamental concurrence between the conservatives and the Socialist Party (SPÖ - Sozialistische Partei Österreichs).

The leading circles of the conservative People's Party (ÖVP - Österreichische Volkspartei), too, considered pure *laissez-faire* outdated, and were ready to accept economic planning at least for a certain period of transition from war to peace. Whereas the Communists seemed to be rather anxious not to frighten the entrepreneurs, the eagerness to intervene in the free market was at greatest with the Social Democrats. But even their radicalism was somewhat limited. If they demanded 'nationalization' or 'socialization', they never had in mind a centrally planned economy of the Soviet type, but a mixed economy within which only the 'commanding heights'[31] should be owned by the state.[32]

In 1945, those heights were for the most part *herrenlos*, in the double sense of the word: ownerless, because their owners were German banks or industrial firms, if not the *Reich* itself, and abandoned, because the managers had left the factories in panic. After the *Anschluß* the Austrian economy had been downright *germanized*. There was hardly any important Austrian enterprise which had not changed hands between 1938 and 1945. The German share in the overall share capital of Austrian joint-stock companies (including banks and insurance companies) had been increased from nine per cent in February 1938 to 57 per cent in 1945.[33]

Since the Austrian authorities had installed *Öffentliche Verwalter* (public administrators) in 1945, there were about 7000 plants formally under public control at the end of 1946. This and the fact that the Allied powers were in the position to claim German external assets as war booty, let both conservatives and social democrats think of nationalization in a very pragmatic manner. Karl Renner, the well-known aged leader of Austrian reformism, therefore could with certain justification call socialization a *Volksnotwendigkeit*, a public necessity and state that it was 'not a matter of principle but a practical imperative'.[34]

After a foundered first attempt to pass a nationalization law in September 1945 the Austrian Parliament finally passed the First Nationalization Act on 26 July 1946, by which 70 firms, plants, and parts of enterprises were taken over by the state.[35] Twenty-nine of them - many of them small oil extracting companies - had been claimed as German assets by the Soviet Union. The Soviet authorities consequently ignored the law and seized the plants in order to reorganize them as USIA (Administration of Soviet Assets in Austria) and SMV (Soviet Oil Administration). Both combines as well as the DDSG (Danube Shipping Company) were run by the Soviets until the State Treaty of 1955 as an extraterritorial complex. According to different calculations, the USIA combine employed 37,000 to 53,000 people in the early fifties, that is 3.5 to 5 per cent of the overall Austrian work force. However, at a regional scale, the role of USIA was more prominent, and its share in the industrial output of Lower Austria may have run up to one-third.[36]

In 1946 Austrian politicians were under pressure of the working class to show some nationalizing attitudes. They had to secure national interests, and they were aware of the fact that only the state and not private Austrian capital could provide the means for reconstructing the ownerless firms. However, state ownership was not the ultimate goal of nationalization, but rather *full employment*. Even socialist economists defined the nationalized industry as the leading sector of reconstruction, providing raw materials, fuel, energy and semi- finished goods at prices well below the world market level.[37] Thus the state-owned firms subsidized the private ones[38] and helped secure employment during the stabilization crisis of 1952.[39] Moreover, they provided an element of political and social stability by 'neutralizing strategic spheres of the Austrian economy'.[40]

At the beginning of the 1950s the share of the nationalized sector in overall industrial employment was about 22 per cent; about one-quarter of the total net value added by Austrian industry fell to the share of the nationalized enterprises. These quotas remained stable until the 1980s, when the nationalized steel industry got caught in a crisis and had to reduce its activities.

4. Austria and the Marshall Plan

The question of the role of the ERP within European postwar economic development has unleashed a long debate between historians.[41] Obviously its significance for *national* reconstruction was by far greater in Austria than in Western Germany and other countries affected by the Second World War (see Table 8.7). The Marshall Plan served, as Eduard März put it, as the 'priming charge' of a 'second take-off period of the Austrian economy'.[42]

Table 8.7 Percentage of national income by ERP aid,
1 July 1948 to 30 June 1949

Country	Percentage
Austria	14.0
Netherlands	10.8
France	6.5
Italy	5.3
Western Germany	2.9
United Kingdom	2.4

Source: Milward, *The Reconstruction of Western Europe*, p. 5.

In general, industry could dip into three main sources of capital investment during the period of reconstruction: self financing, bank credit and the counterpart funds from the Marshall Plan. Unfortunately we can draw only on unadjusted overall investment data covering periods of five to ten years with an average inflation rate of about 40 per cent. But we do know that in key sectors like steel production and power generation there was hardly any investment activity until 1948 (see Table 8.8).

The rate of self-financing seems to have been quite high, especially during the initial period. Its share in total investments amounted to 43 per cent in nationalized industry (including, however, short-term bank credits), and it was even higher in other sectors of the economy. Table 8.9 shows the figures for the industrial combine of the biggest Austrian bank, the state-owned *Creditanstalt-Bankverein* (CA-BV), representing about 7 or 8 per cent of total industrial employment.

Table 8.8 Investment activity of the Austrian iron and steel industry and power companies 1945-50 (nominal value, million AS)

Year	Iron & Steel	Power Companies
1945-46	25.8	n.a.
1947	63.3	17.8
1948	151.8	277.1
1949	262.7	404.3
1950	655.0	470.8

Note: AS - Austrian Schilling

Sources: *Österreichs Grundindustrie verstaatlicht*, Vienna 1951, p. 31; *Zehn Jahre ERP*, p. 67.

Table 8.9 Sources of investment of the industrial combine of the Creditanstalt-Bankverein 1945-51 (million AS at current prices and as %)

Source	AS m	%
Self-financing	416	50.0
Bank credit	146	17.5
Counterpart funds (ERP)	270	32.5
Sum total	832	100.0

Note: AS - Austrian Schilling

Source: Archives of the CA-BV: 'Kommentar zum Johnstone-Bericht 1952'. Unpubl. manuscript, p. 105.

The overall scheme and mechanism of the ERP is well known. Suffice it here to say that Austria received Marshall Plan aid exclusively as grants. The sum total of (direct as well as indirect) ERP aid amounted to about US$956.5 million in the period 1945-55. The bulk of goods imported as direct ERP aid comprised - in contrast to the idea of favouring investment - mainly foodstuffs, whereas capital and semi-finished goods came to only 15 per cent. [43] Until the end of 1949 two thirds of ERP imports comprised foodstuffs, the value of which may be estimated at about $160 million. [44] According to Alan Milward the preponderance of foodstuffs was even greater and amounted to 78 per cent of all ERP shipments still in 1949. [45]

The genial heart of the ERP, however, which really fostered economic recovery were the 'counterpart funds'. They had already been introduced with the Interim Aid (January to July 1948), and were used mainly for investment purposes, as can be seen from Table 8.10; only 15 per cent had to be spent for currency operations, technical aid, stimulation of exports, and 'other purposes'. Between 1949 and 1952 about 30 per cent of total Austrian net investment was contributed by the counterpart funds.[46]

Table 8.10 Expenditure of counterpart funds* in Austria
(million. AS and %) as at 31 March 1955

Purpose	AS m	%
Currency operations	850	6.5
Public investment	2,067	15.9
Industrial investment	6,137	51.8
Agriculture	1,360	10.4
Private housing	554	4.3
Tourism	305	2.3
Technical aid and promotion		
of productivity	296	2.3
Export stimulation	163	1.3
Other purposes	684	5.2
Sum total	13,016	100.0

* Incl. Congress and Interim Aid

Note: AS - Austrian Schilling

Source: Nemschak, *Zehn Jahre*, p. 24.

Thus the Marshall Plan contributed to the high rate of gross investment (15-20 per cent) during the key period (1949-52), a level well above the best interwar year 1929 (10 per cent).[47] And it favoured the public sector: until the end of 1953 about 60 per cent of ERP money went to the state-owned enterprises (power generation, nationalized industries, public transport).[48] In 1948, more than 70 per cent of industrial investment (including power production), carried out within the counterpart funds scheme, were received by state-owned enterprises.[49] Only with the Marshall Plan did the nationalization acts of 1946 and 1947 obtain 'material' ground. This is particularly true for the iron and steel industry and the power generating sector, where - according to a contemporary expert - 'the scarcity of financial means, building material and ... working force [had] paralysed almost every activity' until 1948 (see also Table 8.11).[50]

It was not by accident the power plant of Kaprun became a symbol of reconstruction in Austria. Total investment in Kaprun amounted to 1.8 billion AS in 1947-54 of which 1.3 billion was contributed by ERP funds, roughly 10 per cent of all counterpart means released or one-fifth of the sum total coming to the industrial sector.[51]

Table 8.11 ERP-included investments in the Austrian power generating sector, the iron and steel industry and the nationalized industries as a whole 1948-1954 (as a percentage of total investments)

Year	Power plants	Iron & steel	Overall nationalized industries (b)
1948	35.4	88.4 (c)	-
1949	81.3	-	-
1950	90.5	44.3 (d)	50.8 (e)
1951	77.8	58.1	59.7
1952	65.2	24.7	27.8
1948-1952	72.3	46.4 (f)	46.3 (g)
1953	18.3	32.8	40.1
1954	48.9	11.1	20.7
1945-1954	57.3 (a)	38.9	41.9

Notes: (a) 1947-1954; (b) without electricity; (c) 1947-48; (d) 1949-50; (e) 1945-50; (f) 1947-52; (g) 1945-52

Sources : Österreichs Grundindustrie verstaatlicht, p. 31; März, *Ost und West*, p. 113; *Zehn Jahre ERP*, pp. 67, 75.

It can be alleged that not only the American advisers but also the Austrian side were aware of the (Western) European dimensions of reconstruction: the extension of the steel works at Linz on a large scale has often been regarded as a paradigm of the optimistic spirit of Austrian reconstruction. The dimensions of the plant, however, were such that many experts - having in mind the export stagnation of the interwar years - doubted if it could take advantage of its huge capacities.[52] No wonder that there were repeatedly plans to sell the surplus furnaces abroad until 1947.[53]

The 'traditionalists' (left-wing experts of the WIFO and representatives of the industrial wing of the ÖVP) favoured a Danube instead of the Western orientation related to the Marshall Plan. The most loyal allies of the USA were the social democrats, for economic (they were the promoters of nationaliz-ation) as well as political reasons (they opposed the development in Eastern Europe).

The Sovietization of Eastern Europe cut off Austria's foreign trade with its eastern neighbours in any case after 1948. Between August 1945 and May 1946 Czechoslovakia's share in Austrian external trade still amounted to about forty per cent; even in 1949 that country had remained Austria's third biggest trade partner.[54] However, one has to look at these figures as part of a greater design. Immediately after the war commerce with the neighbouring countries Czechoslovakia, Italy and Switzerland came to two-thirds of Austria's overall foreign trade. In 1951 - under more 'normal' conditions - it had decreased to 18.5 per cent, a share smaller than in 1937.[55] Indeed, as Figure 8.3 indicates, the long run trend (effective at least until 1989) was already clear in 1949.

6. From planning to a free market

One may consider it a particular malice of history that it was precisely under the auspices of the USA that the shaky beginnings of economic planning in Austria were strengthened, culminating in the preparation of a 'national investment plan' for 1950-52, which covered about 90 per cent of public and private investment in order to secure the most rational allocation of Marshall Plan aid. The ultimate goal of planning, however, was the restoration of the market economy. Kurt W. Rothschild therefore saw the postwar years characterized by a 'policy of modifying the basically capitalist process of reconstruction'.[56] Indeed, there had never been any concise planning attempts after the war. But the idea of planning biased the overall attitude of politicians and the process of decision-making. At the very beginning the provisional Renner government (in power until autumn 1945) had already passed several planning laws (which remained on paper only) and had introduced planning institutions (which were never allowed to work at full speed).

There was, for instance, a *Beauftragter für die Industrie* (commissioner for the industry), a left-wing socialist, whose task was to gain an overview of the stock of machinery as a first essential of later planning.[57] The so-called *Kreditlenkungsgesetz* (Act concerning credit regulation) of 2 July 1945 was issued in order to co-ordinate the credit policy of the state and to scrutinize the economic use and urgency of private investments. In other words: in contrast to what had happened after the First World War there existed a certain planning mentality, at least a readiness to accept economic interventionism.

In October 1945 an *Industrieplan* (plan for industry) was accepted at a common conference of the government and the representatives of the (rather conservative-oriented) provinces,[58] which intended a detailed order of resuming production according to the degree of economic use and importance of the respective industries for the reconstruction of other branches.[59] In 1946 - on the advice of the Allied Commission for Austria - a four-year plan for the development of Austrian industry was worked out by the public authorities, which, however, according to the *Gazette of the Allied Commission for Austria* lacked any coherent idea.[60]

Even nationalization was not identical to planning and co-ordination. Until 1948 only the managing boards of the state-owned banks had been constituted. Banks and industrial firms were run in the same decentralized and uncontrolled manner like private enterprises so that a socialist expert resignedly wrote:

> Only in theory we have a nationalized investment goods sector. However, practically, the influence of the government at these enterprises is only a limited one, and the government has ... no possibility to co-ordinate the production plans of the different firms.[61]

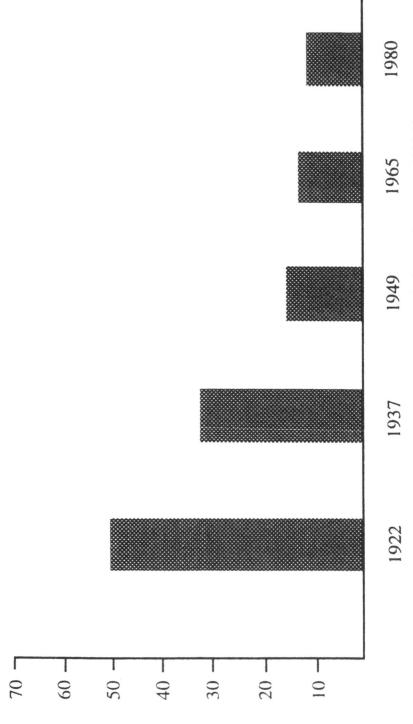

Figure 8.3 Share of the successor states of the former Habsburg Monarchy in Austrian exports, 1922-80

Nevertheless, investment plans and schemes had been worked out to co-ordinate production within single branches, where state influence was great, by a working group of the Ministry of Planning. But only during 1948 were planning activities tightened up with a view to the Marshall Plan, and definitive basic plans were drawn up for the field of power generation, iron and steel, and coal mining.[62] Even the *Kreditlenkungskommission*, which was already dozing at that time, was allowed to go through a time of revival with the Marshall Plan, examining the credit requests of potential borrowers within the counterpart funds scheme.[63]

After the elections of 1949 which brought forth a considerable strengthening of the Socialist Party, more energetic steps were taken in order to control and reorganize the nationalized sector. The state-owned banks, however, came into the sphere of interest of the (ÖVP-controlled) Ministry of Finance and could maintain their autonomous state for the future.

There was never any serious disagreement between the Austrian and American experts concerning the general orientation of economic reconstruction. If we disregard planning of the Soviet type, there were, in principle, two different approaches at hand after 1945: boosting mass consumption (as favoured by the Communist Party and some left-wing economists like Kurt Rothschild), or giving priority to the investment goods sector. The Austrian government was in favour of the second solution already before the Marshall Plan.[64] The lagging behind of the consumer goods industry - only a synonym for the high rate of investment during the period of reconstruction - can be seen from Figure 8.4.

The years 1947-60 can indeed be considered as a second take-off period of the Austrian economy, but a period wholly subordinated to the 'law of disclaiming private consumption'.[65] Nevertheless it laid the foundations for the following decades, when the Austrian economy - after recovery from a short stabilization crisis in 1952-53, caused by the final stabilization of the Austrian currency - was able to grow into a booming world economy. The alarming signs of the structural crisis of the 1960s, which mainly affected the mining and metallurgical sector after the end of the reconstruction boom, were easily (but not finally) concealed by the growth effects from abroad.

Both the Austrians and their foreign partners have contributed to the successful reconstruction of Austria. Both have learned their lessons from interwar history: foreign aid was granted much more 'rationally' and in a more focused way than after the First World War, when the League of Nations had guaranteed the Geneva Loan only after long and fruitless disputes and at conditions unfavourable to Austria. After the Second World War over-all economic reconstruction - not only currency stabilization and balancing the public budget - was at the centre of the debate. Calculated at fixed values, foreign relief and financial aid given to Austria was three to four times higher than after 1918.[66] In other words: the aid was more extensive, was placed at the disposal of the Austrians faster, and used more efficiently than in the interwar period. And it met an Austrian government which recognized the signs of the times and the positive implications of the American offer.

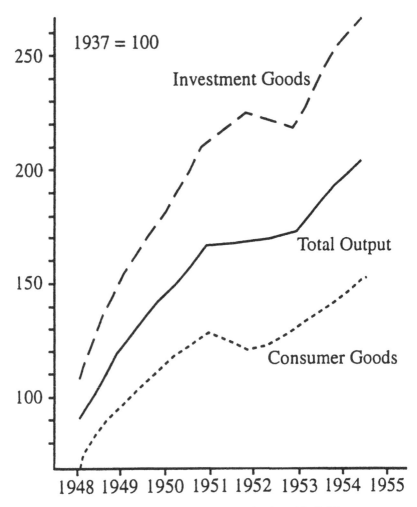

Figure 8.4 Index of Austrian industrial production, 1948-55

Even if the Austrians had merely been lucky in getting into a fair weather period of the world economy, if - in other words - the Austrian development were just a mirror picture of a much greater design, the rather favourable position which Austria has been able to defend until today, has a great deal to do with the way in which it met the challenge of the first post-war decade.

Notes

1   Haberler, G. 'Austria's 'Economic Development after the Two World
     Wars: A Mirror Picture of the World Economy', in: Sven W. Arndt, (ed.)
     (1979), *The Political Economy of Austria*, Washington-London, pp. 61-
     75.

2   Rothschild, K.W. 'Wurzeln und Triebkräfte der Entwicklung der
     österreichischen Wirtschaftsstruktur', in: Weber, W. (ed.), (1961),
     Österreichs Wirtschaftsstruktur gestern-heute-morgen, vol. 1. West
     Berlin, pp. 88-89.

3   Nemschak, F. (1955), *Zehn Jahre österreichische Wirtschaft 1945-1955*.
     Vienna, p.66.

4   The crop of 1945, for example, amounted to about 50 per cent of that of
     1937. See: Rothschild, K.W. (1950), *The Austrian Economy since 1945*.
     London-New York, pp. 26-30.

5   Cf. Kranzelmayer, F. (1959), 'Die Wirtschaftsstruktur Niederösterreichs
     und die Entwicklung seiner Wirtschaft seit Beendigung des Zweiten
     Weltkrieges'. Unpubl. Diss. (Hochschule für Welthandel), Vienna, pp.
     97-98. Also Böck-Greissau, J. C. (1950), 'Die Industrie in Wien,
     Niederösterreich und Burgenland' in: *Festschrift zum fünfzigjährigen
     Bestand der Zeitschrift 'Die Industrie'*. Vienna, p. 41.

6   *Monatsberichte des Österr. Institutes für Wirtschaftsforschung* (WIFO) 1-
     6/1946, pp. 18-21; 7-9/1946.

7   Nemschak, *Zehn Jahre*, p. 40; Cf. (1947), *Österreichisches Jahrbuch
     1945-1946*. Vienna, pp. 329-34.

8   WIFO 1-3/1947, pp. 1-2; Maddison, A. (1976), 'Economic Policy and
     Performance in Europe, 1913-1970' in: Cipolla, C. M. (ed.), *The
     Fontana Economic History of Europe*, vol. 5/2, p. 472

9   Butschek, F. (1985), *Die österreichische Wirtschaft im 20. Jahrhundert*.
     Vienna, p. 107; Schausberger, N. (1970), *Rüstung in Österreich 1938-
     1945*. Vienna, p. 185.

10   Cf. (1983), *Zehn Jahre ERP in Österreich 1948-1958*. Vienna, pp. 88-89;
     Otto Klambauer, Die USIA-Betriebe in Niederösterreich. Vienna, (1958),
     p. 76.

11   To be sure, the French occupation force also favoured and carried out
     dismantling in Tyrol and Vorarlberg, the extent of which, however,
     proved to be much less serious than in Eastern Austria. Cf. Lettner, L.
     (1980), 'Die französische Österreichpolitik von 1943 bis 1946', Unpubl.
     Phil. Diss. Salzburg.

12   Böck-Greissau, *Industrie*, p. 41.

13   Klambauer, *USIA-Betriebe*, pp. 4-25; WIFO 1-6/1946, pp. 79-80, 1-
     3/1947, pp. 29-30, 8/1947, p. 179; Vas, O. (1956), *Wasserkraft- und*

142

Elektrizitätswirtschaft in der Zweiten Republik. Vienna, pp. 14-15.

14 WIFO 1-6/1946, p. 79. Dismantling with similar effects was also reported for the Böhler works at Kapfenberg (Styria).

15 Cf. Abelshauser, W. (1983) *Wirtschaftsgeschichte der Bundesrepublik Deutschland 1945-1980.* Frankfurt/Main, pp. 40-45.

16 WIFO 1-2/1945, p. 30.

17 WIFO 1-2/1945, pp. 10-11, 30-31; 1-6/1946, pp. 26-28.

18 WIFO 1-2/1945, pp. 18-21.

19 Cf. WIFO 1-2/1945, pp. 28-30; 1-6/1946, pp. 95-100.

20 During the period August 1945 - May 1946, 16 per cent of the overall Austrian exports consisted of magnesite. Before 1938 the share of magnesite in exports amounted to less than one per cent. Cf. WIFO 1-6/1946, p. 99.

21 Cf. Abelshauser, *Wirtschaftsgeschichte*, pp. 36-37.

22 WIFO 10-12/1946, p. 172. At this point the Austrian government discussed a barter deal with Czechoslovakia: the steel works at Linz were to sell furnaces in exchange for Czech coal. Cf. Einwitschläger, A. (1986), *Amerikanische Wirtschaftspolitik in Österreich 1945-1949.* Vienna-Cologne-Graz, pp. 45-46.

23 After the war the money supply amounted to approximately nine billion RM as against 1.6 billion in 1937 (according to the official exchange rate of 1 RM = 1.50 AS). Cf. Butschek, *Wirtschaft*, pp. 75-76.

24 Nemschak, *Zehn Jahre*, p. 72: 'Inflation was so to speak officially controlled'.

25 Cf. Prader, H. (1975), 'Probleme kooperativer Gewerkschaftspolitik. Am Beispiel der Politik des ÖSB im Wiederaufbau 1945-1951'. Unpubl. Phil. Diss. University of Salzburg.

26 Cf. Weber, F. (1986), *Der Kalte Krieg in der SPÖ. Koalitionswächter, Pragmatiker und Revolutionäre Sozialisten 1945-1950.* Vienna, pp. 115-119.

27 Shell, K.L. (1969), *Jenseits der Klassen? Österreichs Sozialdemokratie seit 1934.* Vienna-Frankfurt-Zürich, p. 223.

28 Leichter, O. 'Die Tradition der illegalen Bewegung' in: *Zukunft* 7/1948, p. 143.

29 Cf. Weber, F. (1988), 'Zwischen Marx und Keynes. Die wirtschaftspolitische Diskussion der österreichischen Sozialisten und Gewerkschafter 1934-1945' in: Maderthaner, W. and Gruber H. (eds), *Labor in Retreat.* Vienna, pp. 69-105.

30 During the interwar period many Austrian politicians as well as economic experts had doubted the 'viability' of Austria. Cf. Schausberger, N. (1978), *Der Griff nach Österreich*, Vienna-Munich, pp. 81-87.

31 The term was already coined in 1919 by the Austrian socialist leader Otto

Bauer, whose ideas were still alive in 1945. Cf. März, E. & Weber, F. (1979), 'Verstaatlichung nach dem Ersten und Zweiten Weltkrieg' in: *Austriaca*, special issue November, pp. 85-117.

32 Cf. Hollerer, S. (1974), *Verstaatlichung und Wirtschaftsplanung in Österreich (1946-1949)*. Vienna; Deutsch, R. (1978), *Geschichte der Verstaatlichung in Österreich.* 2 vols. Vienna.

33 Cf. Klambauer, O. (1978), 'Die Frage des Deutschen Eigentums in Österreich' in: *Jahrbuch für Zeitgeschichte*, p. 148.

34 Cited in Zimmermann, H. (1983), 'Wirtschaftsentwicklung in Österreich 1945-51 am Beispiel der Lohn-Preis-Abkommen und des Marshallplans'. Unpubl. Phil. Diss. University of Vienna, p. 43.

35 A second nationalization law followed 1947. It concerned only the power-supply companies.

36 Klambauer, *USIA-Betriebe*, pp. 45-46.

37 Cf. Migsch, A. (1948), statement at the 1947 party meeting of the SPÖ. *Protokoll des Parteitages der SPÖ 1947*. Vienna, pp. 159-161.

38 Cf. März, E. (1965), *Österreichs Wirtschaft zwischen Ost und West*. Vienna-Frankfurt-Zürich, pp. 65-83.

39 Whereas employment decreased at an overall rate of 12.3 per cent, it was kept almost stable (-0.3 per cent) in the nationalized sector. Cf. Lacina, F. (1976), 'Verstaatlichung in Österreich' in: *Wirtschaft und Politik. Festschrift für Fritz Klenner*. Vienna, p. 277.

40 Lacina, F. 'Vorwort' in: Deutsch, *Verstaatlichung*, p. 4.

41 Cf. among others: Haberl, O.N. & Niethammer, L. (1986), *Der Marshall-Plan und die europäische Linke*. Frankfurt/Main; Milward, A. S. (1984), *The Reconstruction of Western Europe 1945-51*. London; Maier, C. S. & Bischof, G. (eds), (1992), *Deutschland und der Marshall-Plan*. Baden-Baden.

42 März, *Ost und West*, p.114.

43 Korn, M. (1976), *Das ERP aus österreichischer Sicht 1948-1962*. Vienna, p.109.

44 Source of calculation: Nemschak, *Zehn Jahre*, p. 23; *Zehn Jahre ERP*, p. 91.

45 Milward, *Reconstruction*, p. 103, Table 19.

46 Hofbauer, H. (1992), *Westwärts. Österreichs Wirtschaft im Wiederaufbau*. Vienna, p. 152.

47 WIFO, *Österreichs Volkseinkommen 1913-1963*, pp. 17-19

48 Langer, *Die Verstaatlichungen in Österreich*, p. 275.

49 Sources of calculation: Nemschak, *Zehn Jahre*, p. 30; *Zehn Jahre ERP*, pp. 67, 75.

50 Vas, *Wasserkraft*, p. 13-50

51 Ibid., p. 25.

[52] Cf. März, E. & Szecsi, M. (1982), 'Stagnation und Expansion. Eine vergleichende Analyse der wirtschaftlichen Entwicklung in der Ersten und Zweiten Republik' in: *Wirtschaft und Gesellschaft*. 2, pp. 232-33

[53] Einwitschläger, *Amerikanische Wirtschaftspolitik.*, pp. 45-46.

[54] WIFO 1-6/1946, p. 98; *Statistik des österreichischen Außenhandels für 1949.* pp. 5-6

[55] WIFO 1-3/47, p. 36; (1946) *Österreichs Außenhandel in der Zeit zwischen den beiden Weltkriegen*, Vienna, p. 75-82; *Der österreichische Außenhandel im Jahre 1951*, pp. 8, 10.

[56] Rothschild, *Wurzeln*, p. 129.

[57] Some hints about the activities of this left-wing socialist, Stanislaus Stegu, can be found in documents published by Rathkolb, O. (ed.), (1985), *Gesellschaft und Politik am Beginn der Zweiten Republik*, Vienna-Cologne-Graz.

[58] The *Länderkonferenzen* of 1945 brought together (more conservative) western provinces and the Renner government in Vienna. They played a decisive role in the maintenance of Austria's unity.

[59] Butschek, *Wirtschaft*, p.79.

[60] Cited by Zimmermann, *Wirtschaftsentwicklung*, p. 63.

[61] Süßmayer, K. (1948), 'Die Umstellung unserer Eisen- und Stahlproduktion' in: *Zukunft* 1, p. 21.

[62] Cf. Hollerer, *Verstaatlichung*, pp. 168-187.

[63] 'Kommentar zum Johnstone-Bericht'. pp. 101-102.

[64] Cf. Zimmermann, *Wirtschaftsentwicklung*, pp. 242-250.

[65] Vodopivec, A. (1966), *Die Balkanisierung Österreichs. Folgen einer großen Koalition*, Vienna-Munich, p. 16.

[66] Weber, F. (1987), 'Österreichs Wirtschaft in der Rekonstruktionsperiode nach 1945' in: *Zeitgeschichte*, 14/7, p. 294

CHAPTER NINE

Property Rights and Debt in East-West European Relations*

Michael C. Kaser

Eastern Europe in the last months of the 1980s regained its human rights; the task of the 1990s has been equitably to restore property rights. The historian, like the philosopher or the theologian, may consider whether and where to place property rights among human rights, but the economist sees them as a means, not an end. That end is the efficient allocation of scarce resources among limitless demands, currently and over generations: it is better served by a flexible market than by any other mechanism we know. A mixture of private and public ownership fuels that mechanism better than exclusivity at either extreme.

In no century but our own have property rights undergone such swingeing changes. I shall begin therefore with a rough calibration of the world's assets held privately and publicly. Co-operatives are - perhaps arbitrarily - classed as private under market regimes and as state-run under central planning. The shape of the century's time-series is obvious - the private sector dominant in 1900, falling to an all-time low in mid-century, and rapidly rising now.

Later I turn to international transactions in those property rights - conventionally in markets for goods, for labour and for capital. Very tentatively I try to quantify the annual values of each and thence their relative ranking over time. For Europe as a whole the order of 1900 - labour, followed by goods, with capital last - has lately been reversed - capital, goods and now labour last. But in contemporary East-West European relations the first two are transposed - the flow of goods is much greater than that of capital - and international labour transfer is not only bottom but much further below the other two than among Western countries.

An explanation of the low level of East-West goods and capital flow constitutes my third section. The East European countries as a group, though not the USSR, were structural debtors throughout the century. Western ownership of Eastern assets or Eastern indebtedness to the West would, under market conditions, have increased *pari passu* with the current deficit. I show how this was indeed the case by 1930: foreign-held assets equalled an astounding 70 per cent of GNP in Hungary, Romania and Yugoslavia - compared with 6 per cent in contemporary Italy, a not dissimilar economy.[1] I then trace the moratoria, repudiations and expropriations which cancelled the property rights concerned.

Finally, I examine the restitution of East-West capital flow which began in the 1970s with a combination of Western bank liquidity (attributable particularly to the deposit of OPEC-member balances) and Eastern hopes for 'import-led growth'. Caught short by the rescheduling crisis of 1982, interest-bearing credit first declined and then rose only modestly. The privatization and marketization following the 1989 revolutions in Eastern Europe, and which are now likely in the USSR, should attract the equity capital which the uncompetitive economies of the East so badly need.

I said I would begin by documenting the ebb and flow of private ownership. The twentieth century began at the extreme which Adam Smith advocated - the dominance of private property exercised in little-constrained markets for goods, capital and labour. The First World War added more constraints, notably in the German *Kriegswirtschaft*, which Lenin took as a model for the state planning of production and distribution. But neither the Central Powers nor the Allies displaced as proprietor the individual or the joint-stock company. The expansion of the role of the state in the first quarter-century was, rather, in the interests of the civilian economy. The German and Japanese governments had never embraced *laissez-faire* as thoroughly as had the British, and countries industrializing even later made still greater use of state intervention. Such policies were especially to the fore in Russia before the October Revolution, and in Eastern Europe after Versailles. Witte's state support for industry and transport, and the promotion of cartels are classic examples; Stolypin's land reform was arguably the biggest transfer of property rights anywhere in the decade before the First World War.

Two widespread populist claims that were unleashed by the end of the First World War - social justice and nationalism - had an effect on property rights, but hardly shifted the continent's median between private and public. Land reform was total and immediate in the newly-created but still fragile Soviet Russia. Lenin sought by an alliance (*smychka*) with a property-owning peasantry to neutralize their political conservatism - just as Stolypin sought by his land reform to harness their conservatism. Most country folk had voted for the Social Revolutionaries in the Constituent Assembly which the Bolsheviks dispersed with bayonets. In East Europe land reform was as much, but more peaceably, dominated by political considerations. Land reform in Yugoslavia and Romania destroyed all large holdings, but only pruned a few big estates in Poland, Hungary and Czechoslovakia. Bulgaria was already a land of small peasants but enacted a reform none the less.

Ownership change for non-farm assets was initially huge in Soviet Russia: under 'war communism' virtually everything was expropriated. A myriad of small enterprises were soon handed back as the 'New Economic Policy' began, and as the Soviet government normalized relations with Western states at Genoa and Rapallo. The Treaties of Versailles, Trianon and Saint-Germain allowed the allied states, Czechoslovakia, Poland, Romania and Yugoslavia, to 'nostrify' the assets of ex-enemy nationals (Austrian, German or Hungarian) - that is to pass ownership to their own nationals or registered companies. The state was the main beneficiary of nostrification in the capital markets of Romania and Yugoslavia; domestic companies took over most affected assets in Czechoslovakia but in Poland many German proprietors remained in beneficial ownership through Swiss or other nominees. The Romanian state intervened in the labour market to require that subsidized enterprises employ a work force at least three-quarters of whom were Romanian nationals. Programmes of 'state-encouraged' enterprise were also pursued in Bulgaria and Yugoslavia. Industrialists in the Czech Lands were well represented in the new Czechoslovak state and preferred independence to intervention. But many less efficient Slovak firms were bankrupted as their previously protected markets under the Hungarian Crown were riven by the new frontiers. The Depression punctured Czech confidence but the state still relied on the industrialists and made its chief device compulsory cartelization. The economic role of the state in the 1930s was greatest in Poland - the four-year investment plan of 1936 was intended to create a whole new industrial region - but the Hungarian Györ Programme (1938-43), otherwise the 'billion pengö investment plan', ran it close.

Such plans, launched by right-wing, military-dominated governments, were reverberations both from the Schacht policies of Nazi Germany and from the five-year plans of Stalin. Both these powers by the mid-1930s had authoritarian economies but Nazi Germany retained and exploited private property. It was the completion of nationalization and collectivization in the USSR which abruptly steepened the century's gradient towards state property rights.

I want to return at the end to the Communist Party's linkage of political monopoly and property monopsony, but at the present point of my argument the issue is only of the degree of state ownership on the world scale.

The twenty years to 1950 were decisive. Under the first five-year plan, 1928-32, Stalin's USSR shut down the market for goods by ending the New Economic Policy: by its drive to self-sufficiency in a closed economy; by collectivization; and by the liquidation of private retailing. The labour market was restricted by the issuance of residence-tied internal passports and by control of recruitment under central manpower planning. Capital markets were closed by nationalizing the remainder of industry; by the prohibition of mercantile credit within a monobank system; by the inconvertibility of the rouble; and by the eviction of foreign concessions. One remains astonished at the speed of imposition of the 'administrative-command system', as its Soviet critics came pejoratively to describe it.

The war economy of both Allied and Axis Powers restricted market forces everywhere between 1939 and 1945, and many post-war governments in Europe and Asia warded off any return. Notable within the state-oriented trend in market economies were the Attlee government's nationalizations in Britain, Monnet's Commissariat au Plan in France and Mahalanobis's planning under the Nehru administration in India. The maverick exceptions included the West German *Sozialmarktwirtschaft* and the Belgian *économie mixte*. The Director of the Moscow Institute of World Economy was led to remark in 1947 that Britain had 'a kind of Gosplan'. Quantitatively more comprehensive in their termination of private property were the communist regimes installed between 1945 and 1949 in eight states of Eastern Europe, in

China and in North Korea. Even the communist government in Mongolia installed as long ago as 1921 did not nationalize or run a central plan until 1947.

Exactly halfway through the century, therefore, more than two-fifths of the earth's population lived under an ideology of the exclusivity of state ownership of the means of production. One of Lenin's first decrees 'On Land' prohibited the private ownership of land, but in East Europe an early act of the post-1945 governments was to eliminate 'landlessness' by resolute land reform. Later, however, in all those states save Poland and Yugoslavia formal proprietorship or usufruct was overlaid by state-dominated co-operatives or communes. Yugoslavia in 1950 replaced state by worker management but private capital had no more than a toehold until the reforms of 1988 and 1990.

The median on a world calibration of property rights remained fairly stable in the three ensuing decades, pushed a little to the left by a proclivity to state ownership or 'parastatals' in Africa and parts of Latin America, and to the right by the sheer augmentation of the private sector in North America, Japan and East Asia. In the 1980s the gradient has tipped definitively towards the private end. A few months, December 1978 to May 1979, separated two turning-points - Deng Xiaoping's leadership of China and the first of Margaret Thatcher's three election victories. Wildly different their privatization objectives might be but they 'rolled back the state' none the less. Republican victories in the US Presidential elections and those of the CDU/CSU in the Federal Republic, the enlargement and deepening of the European Community, the Tokyo Round and the Uruguay Round have all been in step with the globalization of the market. Quantum leaps in the scale of information processing and in the speed of its communication supported the new world-wide corporate ethos.

From this, of course, the USSR and its six Eastern European allies remained cocooned. Their state monopoly practice and their protectionism within CMEA can be shown to have been actually efficiency-reducing, not merely making productivity growth slower than under capitalism. Two examples may suffice. General factor productivity was negative in the USSR from around 1970[2] when, frightened by the association of political with economic liberalization in the Prague Spring they had just suppressed, the Soviet leadership reversed the modest managerial decentralization of 1965. The productivity index had been positive under Khrushchev's and Kosygin's devolutions. A second instance is in intra-industry trade,[3] the measure of which is the extent to which an export of a narrowly defined commodity group (usually SITC at the three-digit level) is offset by imports of the same. Not only was the index lower in East-East and East-West trade than in West-West trade, but for the same commodity membership of CMEA is a good explanatory variable for a lower index value.

Proof of a much diminished economic performance in comparison with enterprise under market stimuli would not of itself have shifted communist governments towards restoration of private ownership but it sapped confidence in central planning. From the mid-1960s to the eve of the cataclysm of 1989 they essayed innumerable, but very limited, reforms. The failure of those reforms and an international 'Duesenberry Effect' ('try to keep up with your neighbours - that is, the West's consumption') were surely factors. So was the increasing encroachment of military requirements on civilian technological innovation and on investment at large. But the necessary conditions were inevitably political, headed by Mikhail Gorbachev's election in 1985 must be the most important. Andropov had abortively launched *perestroika* (*his* word) in 1983 and, like Gorbachev, confined its remit to the economy. It was only in early 1987 that Gorbachev extended the policy to the governance of the country. Without that political revolution and devolution the Soviet legislature would never have permitted the collective or state farmer to lease land to till on a household basis. Nor would it have enacted equality before the law of all forms of property or put the legal provisions of privatization in place.

Causal analysis of the East European revolutions is for the political scientist today and for the historian tomorrow, but they have rendered definitive the availability of state-run assets to private and corporate owners. As the century closed, the median on the property scale moves nearer to its starting point.

Smaller swings have taken place in earlier centuries and with profound consequences - in Leuven industrial decline followed the mass emigration of the weavers after the nobles swung the balance of property rights in their own favour in 1382. The twentieth century is distinguished by the sheer magnitude of the change, not only in aggregate within the spectrum from private to public, as I have just sought to sketch, but also in the composition of the markets in which those property rights are exercised. My account of the aggregative shifts used the conventional division into markets for goods, for labour and for capital. Few doubt the welfare gains which market-clearing prices generate for current transactions in goods and services. But there were serious social choices to be made in the two other markets, which vexed the peoples and governments of East Europe. There was job security to be weighed against the risk of unemployment and a widening of income differentials. There was subsidized investment making goods for subsidized consumers which had to be set against a variable market for capital from which a few get super-profits and others are bankrupted. Some East European governments made such a choice before - albeit on a smaller scale - when in the late 1930s they lent clearing balances to Nazi Germany to ensure employment at home. But that I must touch upon later.

During the twentieth century the ranking of the three markets - of goods, of labour and of capital - has been reversed. On the eve of the First World War the value of Europe's emigrants working in other continents was about equal to Europe's total exports:[4] if migration within Europe is added, the labour market outranked the goods market, which in turn outstripped Europe's transnational capital flow. In the last decade of this century, the international capital market is much bigger than the export of goods while the transnational labour market is the smallest.

In East-West flows the relative magnitudes of the 1980s take on yet another order - goods export first, capital second and labour last. East Europe had provided 80 per cent of United States immigration in the decade or so before the restrictions of 1924 but the region's prewar average of a million overseas migrants a year was halved in the 1920s and both these and migration within Europe were very small in the 1930s. The Soviet authorities halted emigration totally, as did East European communist governments after the Second World War. That war brought labour transfers which cannot be dignified by the name of 'market' - the slavery of East Europeans forced to work elsewhere within the Nazi *Grossraum*. The autarchy of the USSR, CMEA integration and the Western embargo, all within the confrontation of the Cold War, shrank trade while wholesale nationalization eliminated the movement of capital.

In East-West European relations at the end of the communist period, the biggest money numbers are found in trade - in 1989 $42 billion in each direction - but it is a mere 2 per cent of world commerce. The East-West capital flow was $6 billion that year, and payments associated with past or present labour were less than half that sum (emigrant and expatriate remittances and income from intellectual property).[5] But if a labour market is measured as I did for the world - production by emigrants in their host country - the figure is trivial. The communist borders were closed for four decades and those who crossed, legally or illegally, for political asylum were few with respect to the workforce on either side. Now that the political obstacles have crumbled, it is time to consider how all three East-West markets can begin to match the expectations of Easterners and the potential of Westerners.

Bilateralism and currency inconvertibility not only stifle trade but inhibit capital flow. If a country exports as much as it imports it can make the gains which Ricardo discerned, but factor ownership is unaffected. Imbalance must be settled either by ceding property rights or by indebtedness. In the case of an import deficit the foreigner buys land, natural resources or reproducible capital or lends a financial asset. Because East European countries as a group - though not the USSR - were in structural deficit throughout the period, their assets should increasingly have become the property of foreigners. That they did not - foreign equity in 1989 was a mere 1 per cent of East European capital stock - is attributable to state policy beginning with the confiscations, moratoria and forced conversions in the 1930s and 1940s.

Because of those ruptures of property rights, the ratio of gross foreign debt to GNP was much lower in 1989 than it was before the Second World War. It is impractical to go back before the First World War because much of the transfer of ownership or the incurrence of debt took place within large empires and hence did not appear in international accounts. A 1913 ratio for Tsarist Russia is nevertheless instructive:[6] foreign-held assets were the equivalent of 35 per cent of GNP. Much higher ratios were shown for some East European countries on the brink of the 1930 Depression - a staggering 70 per cent in Hungary, Romania and Yugoslavia and nearly 40 per cent in Bulgaria. The other two states had more moderate ratios - 25 per cent in Poland and 15 per cent in Czechoslovakia. But even the lowest was high by the benchmark of 6 per cent in Italy in the late 1920s - a broadly comparable economy. The corresponding ratios of communist government borrowing in the 1970s were less than those of 60 years ago. The 1988 ratios were headed by Yugoslavia (34 per cent), Hungary (28 per cent), followed by Poland (19 per cent) and Bulgaria (15 per cent) but were only 4 per cent in Czechoslovakia; Romania after a fruitless absorption of loans in the 1970s switched in 1982 under what proved to be intolerable pressure from Ceausescu to repay. By early 1989 Romania had eliminated its external debt and had allowed all but one of its joint ventures to wither. Czechoslovakia was the least indebted East European country until its division into two nations. Between the two wars it was the sole surplus country of the region; after the Soviet suppression of 1968 its communist rulers were hyper-cautious in relations with the West.

In both periods Czechoslovakia paid dearly in uncompetitiveness from its foreign-debt policy. Starting independence with half the industrial capacity of the Austro-Hungarian Empire (but only a quarter of the population),[7] Czechoslovakia promoted exports (an annual 11 per cent growth in the mid-1920s) without importing the plant needed for thorough modernization. Instead foreign debt was redeemed, foreign-held shares of domestic firms were repatriated, and sales of foreign currency maintained an overvalued koruna. In the Depression, Czechoslovakia was the hardest and longest hit of all European states: its obsolescent assets were ill-placed to confront rivals' dumping when demand fell. Czechoslovakia was again forced into the same mistake after the communist coup of 1948: it tied its exports to the USSR, overvalued its currency and neglected modernization of its capital stock. In both periods the foreign borrowing that was both feasible and profitable was ignored.

The high ratio of the foreign-held capital stock to that national production flow in the interwar years arose partly as the inheritance of prewar obligations. For the six European states as a group more than half the debt originated before the war. The new Soviet state avoided such commitment by repudiating the totality of Tsarist loans and nationalizing foreign property without compensation. That closed the door on Western capital markets but when a goods market was opened under Lenin's New Economic Policy of 1921, a Soviet delegation at the Genoa Conference of 1922 was prepared to settle all foreign claims prior to 1914 against a resumption of diplomatic relations and of access to Western loans. The agreement faltered on war-time debt and the bigger settlements did not come until Gorbachev's renewal of the opening to Western markets. The East European debt which had accumulated after the First World War was partly for stabilization under League of Nations schemes and partly for development (as also after the Second World War). Then, as now, not all lending achieved its objective and only in three countries (Bulgaria, Hungary and Poland) did it add to net capital stock.

There are further parallels from the banking crises - between the Credit-Anstalt crash of 1931 and Latin American and East European rescheduling of 1982. The consequences of each Western slump were similar: capital movement, like trade, dried up but was not reversed. There was no 'economic Munich', a theory that Western capital withdrew in favour of German funds in the manner that Western governments abandoned Czechoslovakia to Hitler. Hitler's - better, Schacht's - policy sought the reverse flow of funds: it was not Germany that would invest in East Europe, but East Europe in Germany. This was achieved as the Southeast European countries were forced to lend to Nazi Germany through the notorious Reichsmark clearing accounts and became locked into products for which the terms of trade had deteriorated sharply. This export of capital, together with re-armament, 'bought' domestic employment - a trade-off of political importance because the Depression was worse in East Europe than in the West. The fall in trade was deeper and the start of recovery later in East Europe than in the rest of the continent.[8] Trade dependency (exports in GDP) in 1937 was a half to two-thirds that of 1929, save in Romania where it was three-quarters. Low labour costs and policies of import substitutions brought many multinationals into Eastern Europe; through their equity investment they replaced part of what had been lost in credit flow. The Soviet Union reached a nadir in autarchy in 1937 - only 0.5 per cent of GDP was exported - but did not escape Schacht's trap. The USSR, too, lent to Germany its unrequited exports paid in clearing Reichmarks.

During the Second World War East European labour was exploited and its capital stock reduced. But the outcomes varied widely: whereas Poland and the USSR lost about a third of their capital stock, Bulgaria and Czechoslovakia emerged with more capital; Hungary and Yugoslavia suffered substantial loss, Romania less so. These losses evoked some post-war West-East funding, but UNRRA aid was too quickly terminated and Stalin forbade adherence to the Marshall Plan. Western property was expropriated and a combination of Soviet 'mixed companies' and imposed prices made the USSR a net beneficiary of intra-bloc trade. After Stalin's death CMEA's price agreement (Bucharest, 1958) gradually converted the Soviet Union into a donor: during the 1970s the six East European states gained as much from the USSR as they did by the re-admission of Western credits - some $70 billion net from each direction. Such an inflow should have stimulated 'import-led growth'. Western capital goods bought on credit and domestic investment facilitated by cheap primary inputs from the USSR should have modernized plant for the production of competitive exports with which the credits would be repaid. The policy failed, did nothing to remedy systemic dysfunction and led to the debt crisis of 1981-2.

The capital inflow as East Europe denationalizes should be much more productive. Property rights are open to foreign purchases, generating a potential more conducive to growth than debt capital. East European banking systems are being commercialized, but except for IMF stabilization loans or stand-by credits there is no return to blanket 'balance-of-payments' borrowing: flows must either be of equity or of capital for gearing specific enterprises. There is now equity in which to invest, due to privatization and liberalized access to foreign capital.

In no country of the world was denationalization required for so large a share of the national stock. Asset sales offered a wide opportunity for the Western investor, but some were pre-empted by local party or managerial leaders. At the moment of change, popular feeling was thereby aroused, posing questions of whether workers or citizens should be given shares and whether the state should keep natural resources under national ownership. The trade-off of jobs against capital became a salient issue for the new democracies as was the restitution of land ownership.

Overall, the changes in property rights since 1989 involved problems of valuation which exemplify the shortcomings of the Marxist theory of value - state-monopoly management and the disarticulation of domestic from foreign transactions. Some valuations were negative - the cost of rectifying pollution or other environmental damage outweighed the value of the equipment, or the plant was so obsolete as to be uncompetitive without state subsidy.

The issue of asset valuation was but one part of East Europe's monetary problems: on the scale of time or of amplitude the experience of the former states of the USSR and East Europe as a world region is matched only by Latin America. The three variables - prices, exchange rates and monetary disequilibria - have seriously disturbed the transmission mechanism between external and domestic sectors and the structure of entitlements internally.

Price fluctuation has been severe in both directions. Hungary in 1946 still holds the world record for hyper-inflation: the new forint exchanged for an old pengö at ten to the power of 36. Deflation between 1929 and 1933-35 was a halving of wholesale prices in Bulgaria, Poland and Romania: that index was however not a record - Belgium and Japan, for example, did worse - but was hard enough. The trough of the terms of trade in the 1930s slump, like the peak of inflation after the First World War, were common to East Europe and the USSR. When the rouble was finally stabilized in 1924 the new unit exchanged for 50 billion pre-1921 roubles, which was not as bad as the contemporary replacement of 1000 billion Marks for one Reichsmark. The leading economist among Trotsky's supporters, Yevgeny Preobrazhensky, declared at the time that inflation had been 'the machine gun of the Commissariat of Finance, attacking the bourgeois system in the rear and using the currency laws of that system to destroy it'. The circumstances of that often-cited assertion were specific to Soviet 'war communism'. The young Bolshevik leaders were prepared - some were keen - to abolish money altogether. The argument went that the 'veil of money' obscured real relations between exploiters and exploited and was not required when, with no conflicting property interests, there would be neither exploitation nor alienation. Money transactions were no longer needed by an economy, as Lenin put it, operating as 'one big factory': the simplest accounting for inputs and outputs was enough. A draft law of 1920 would have replaced money by 'labour units' (*tredy* in the Russian contraction) but was overtaken by the reintroduction of the market under the New Economic Policy. A disdain for money resurfaced during the first five-year plan when military-style campaigns were in vogue for mobilizing industrial resources and collectivizing agriculture. The ethos and mechanism of Soviet planning were summarized by the Polish economist Oscar Lange as '*sui generis* a war economy'. If the planners' allocation of resources - goods, labour and capital - were by *fiat*, price flexibility was in the Soviet view not only unnecessary but obstructive. Such an attitude towards money, so contrary to that prevailing in market economies, helps us to understand the tolerance shown to the monetary disequilibria which have characterized most years of communist rule anywhere.

Monetary imbalances occur within a market system but under abnormal conditions, which governments usually seek to disperse. The USSR and East Europe have experienced disequilibria under both market and non-market circumstances. Communist governments have often confiscated the inflationary overhang by a currency reform, withdrawing the old at a sharp discount to the new. Examples are the USSR in 1947, and Poland, Bulgaria and Romania between 1950 and 1952. Implicit confiscation took place in East Germany when holdings of Ostmarks up to certain limits were exchanged at one to one Deutschmark, but above those limits at two to one. The Bolshevik cancellation of Tsarist obligations was the equivalent of about half net material product and the state loan put under moratorium in 1957 was about half annual personal disposable income (perhaps a better comparison because there were no institutional subscribers as for Tsarist public debt).

East European governments after each world war had to protect their monetary systems not only from inflation but so as to adjust to new frontiers. Czechoslovakia, Poland, Romania and Yugoslavia had to knit together the various currencies of previous national administrations and occupation authorities. Each stabilization in each postwar period, as well as the war-time monetary disorders, are a history in themselves, but in some states the time taken to return to normality was much longer than in Western Europe. Thus the stabilization after 1918 of the Romanian leu took until 1929, and of the Yugoslav dinar until 1931 - ironically only a few days before the Credit-Anstalt collapse which signalled a new round of instability. The stabilization of the leu after the Second World War was also especially prolonged: Romania suffered the second worst inflation of the region and the final state of reform took place only in 1952.

Following stabilization all the East European states, by then under communist rule, determined upon rigid administered pricing, both wholesale and retail. Repressed inflation undermined incentives, not quite along the path of the Barro-Grossman negative labour-supply multiplier, but akin to it, and the labour market was distorted. The twin evils of chronic excess demand and chronic shortage brought severe disequilibrium to household income and outlay, to enterprise finance and to the public accounts. The goods market was seriously unbalanced. Finally, the isolation of domestic prices from the relativities of world market prices led to multiple exchange rates - at the worst as many rates as there were traded goods - and total inconvertibility. Governments could only engage in the world capital market at arm's length: no automatic transmission mechanism existed.

All the countries of Eastern Europe need, in the post-communist decade of the century, need a huge inflow of Western funds for modernization to render their capital stock competitive and to offset balance-of-payments deficits. Western governments are helping - bilaterally, through the European Community and the European Bank for Reconstruction and Development and through membership of international economic organizations, but the opening up of property rights allows private capital the bigger part. As the economies have embraced full choice among property rights within stable macro-frameworks, there is no need for the concept of 'East-West relations' as the century closes.

Notes

* Based on opening address to the 1990 Congress of the International Economic History Association, Leuven, Belgium.

1 Assets in GNP: see note 6.

2 General factor productivity: author's calculations drawn partly from CIA,*Handbook of Economic Statistics*.

3 Intra-industry trade: doctoral research by J. Lisiecki.

4 Emigration 1891-1914 was 24m (from Thomas, B. in: Thomas, B. (ed.), (1958), *Economics of International Migration*. London, p. 4), generating at least the equivalent of the UK per capita GNP of £60.7 (Schremmer, D. (1989), in: *Cambridge Economic History of Europe*. Vol.. VIII, p. 354), converted at $4.87 to £ in 1914 = $295 per capita. As 54 per cent had gone to the United States (Thomas, *loc. cit.*) the total generated is likely to be higher (Bairoch, P. (1989), in: *Cambridge Economic History of Europe*. Vol. VIII, p. 3 shows US relationship to UK; his figures are for all 1913 populations - per capita GNP was 1.32 times that of the UK). Their product was at least $7 bn.
Exports in 1910 were $8.7 bn (Bairoch *loc. cit,*).
Gross foreign lending by 1913 was $38.7 bn from Europe, $44 bn from all sources (Thomas, B. in Adler, J.H. (ed.), (1967), *Capital Movements and Economic Development.*, p. 10). In 1989 international equity flows totalled $2 trillion (Howell, M. & Cozzina, A. (1990), *International Equity Flows*. Salomon Bros, London. Total world exports in 1988 were $2.7 trillion (1989), GATT, *International Trade 1988-89*, Vol. II, Geneva, p. 3. Labour position impressionistic, awaiting more research. East-West flows: trade 1989 from ECE, (1990), *Economic Survey of Europe in 1989-1990*. New York, pp. 411-2; capital flow from (1990), *International Banking and Financial Market Developments*. Bank for International Settlements, Basle, August, p. 7. Percentage of migrants after 1910 to US who were European from Hauner, M. in: Kaser, M. & Radice, E.A. (eds), *Economic History of Eastern Europe 1919-1975*, Vol. 2, p. 88. East European migration pre- and inter-war from *ibid.*, pp. 86-8.

5 Remittances etc. (net services less investment income) from ECE, *op. cit.*, p. 20.

6 Tsarist Russian foreign-held assets from Bovykine, V. (1989), 'Les Emprunts russes a l'étranger', paper to International Colloquium on Foreign Loans, Debt and Economic Development in the Nineteenth and Twentieth Centuries. Campinas, Brazil July: Table 1 shows 75.85 million roubles for 1913: Gregory, P.R. (1982), *Russian national Income 1885-1913*, p. 57 shows NMP in 1913 as 20,266 million roubles and cites Bergson, A. on p. 109 as giving depreciation as 1040 million roubles on

an NMP of 15,570 million roubles in 1928. The same 6.6 per cent is added to Gregory's 1913 NNP to yield a GNP 1913 of 21,604 billion roubles. East European debt ratio from Notel, R. in: Kaser & Radice, (1986), *op. cit.*, Vol. II, p. 233, except for Yugoslavia from Berend, I. 'Foreign Capital and the Socialist Economies of Central-East Europe after World War II'. Campinas, Brazil, p. 3. GNP per capita from Lethbridge, E. in: Kaser & Radice, *op. cit.*, Vol. I, p. 538. Italy from Storaci, M. & Tatara, G. 'Some Problems Relating to External Finance in Italy during the Twenties'. Campinas, p. 20. 1988 ratios from gross debt in ECE, *op. cit.*, p. 204 applied to GNP from OECD, (1990), *Economic Outlook.* June.

7   Czechoslovak capacity as share of Austro-Hungarian Empire from Myant, M., review of Teichova, A. (1989), *The Czechoslovak Economy 1918-1970* in: *International Affairs.* p. 615; population of Czechoslovakia from Hauner, p. 76; Empire from Bairoch, *loc. cit.*.; growth of exports from Drabek, Z. in: Kaser & Radice, loc. cit. Share of pre- and postwar debt from Nötel, *op. cit.* p. 224.

8   Trade dependency in East Europe, from Hauner in: Kaser & Radice, *op. cit.*, p. 468.

Index

For Product Safety Concerns and Information please contact our EU
representative GPSR@taylorandfrancis.com Taylor & Francis Verlag GmbH,
Kaufingerstraße 24, 80331 München, Germany

Printed and bound by CPI Group (UK) Ltd, Croydon, CR0 4YY
08/05/2025
01864412-0011